LEBANON

Sean Sheehan & Zawiah Abdul Latif

Marshall Cavendish
Benchmark
New York

PICTURE CREDITS

Cover photo: © char abunmansoor/Alamy
alt.TYPE/Reuters: 28, 29, 31, 34, 36, 52, 55, 58, 63, 68, 69, 87, 89, 105 • Bes Stock: 5, 18, 40, 48, 67, 74, 84, 85
Corbis Inc: 32, 85, 90,92, 95, 124,126 • Eye Ubiquitous/Hutchison: 12 • Getty Images: 62, 114 • Lonely Planet Images: 13 •
Photolibrary: 1, 4, 6, 9, 14, 16, 17, 22, 23, 30, 38, 41, 42, 43, 46, 50, 51, 53, 54, 56, 59, 60, 61, 65, 70, 71, 73, 76, 77, 78, 79, 80,
81, 84, 88, 91, 94, 100, 102, 106, 108, 112, 113, 114, 117, 118, 122, 125, 126, 129

PRECEDING PAGE

A young Lebanese performer in her costume during a festival in Beirut, Lebanon.

Publisher (U.S.): Michelle Bisson
Editors: Deborah Grahame, Mabelle Yeo, Crystal Ouyang, Sylvy Soh
Copyreader: Daphne Hougham
Designers: Jailani Basari, Lock Hong Liang
Cover picture researcher: Connie Gardner
Picture researchers: Thomas Khoo, Joshua Ang

Marshall Cavendish Benchmark
99 White Plains Road
Tarrytown, NY 10591
Web site: www.marshallcavendish.us

© Times Media Private Limited 1997
© Marshall Cavendish International (Asia) Private Limited 2008
All rights reserved. First edition 1997. Second edition 2008.
® "Cultures of the World" is a registered trademark of Times Publishing Limited.

Originated and designed by Times Media Private Limited
An imprint of Marshall Cavendish International (Asia) Private Limited
A member of Times Publishing Limited

All Internet sites were correct and accurate at the time of printing. All monetary figures in this publication are in U.S. dollars.

Library of Congress Cataloging-in-Publication Data
Sheehan, Sean, 1951–
    Lebanon / by Sean Sheehan and Zawiah Abdul Latif. — 2nd. ed.
      p. cm. — (Cultures of the world)
    Summary: "Provides comprehensive information on the geography, history, wildlife, governmental structure, economy, cultural
      diversity, peoples, religion, and culture of Lebanon"—Provided by publisher.
    Includes bibliographical references and index.
      ISBN 978-0-7614-2081-1
    1. Lebanon—Juvenile literature. I. Latif, Zawiah Abdul. II. Title. III. Series.
    DS80.S53 2007
    956.92—dc22   2006101735

Printed in China

9 8 7 6 5 4 3 2 1

CONTENTS

These curiously shaped rocks, otherwise known as the Pigeon Rocks, are found off the coast of Beirut.

A national celebration taking place in Beirut's city square.

INTRODUCTION

LEBANON, whose name is derived from the Semitic root word *laban*—meaning "white," in reference to its snowcapped mountains—was once part of Greater Syria before its partition into Syria, Lebanon, and Palestine. Renowned for its sophistication, culture, trade, and conflict, this small but influential state has been shaped by at least 12 different civilizations, going back to the era of the Phoenicians, who created the world's first commercial empire. Lebanon's dynamic cultural diversity has, ironically, given rise to many ethnic and religious conflicts throughout the ages. In 1975 a civil war started that lasted 15 years and tore Lebanon's economy and society apart.

Present-day Lebanon still faces major challenges in its push toward political stability, social solidarity, and economic and environmental sustainability for national reconstruction. All these must be achieved in the face of a fragile Lebanese identity, diverging interests of numerous religious communities and political factions, wide socioeconomic disparities, and the problem of foreign interference. Nevertheless, Lebanon is blessed with creativity and entrepreneurship, and it has slowly emerged as a financial, commercial, and recreational center of the Middle East.

LEBANON IS A COUNTRY at the eastern end of the Mediterranean Sea. Its total land area is 4,036 square miles (10,453 square km), a little smaller than Connecticut. It is bordered by Syria on the north and the east, by Israel in the south, and on the west, the Mediterranean Sea. The total length of Lebanon's land border is 282 miles (454 km), of which 49 miles (79 km) are shared with Israel and 233 miles (375 km) with Syria. Lebanon's coastline stretches for 140 miles (225 km).

Above and opposite: **Mountains in Lebanon are within easy reach. Buildings hug the slopes and sheep use bridges carved by nature.**

REGIONS

Lebanon is a small land with notable geographical contrasts. Like any mountainous country, Lebanon's topography and terrain, climate, soils, and vegetation differ markedly within short distances. There are four regions with distinctive features of their own.

COASTAL PLAIN The coastal plain from Tripoli in the north down to Beirut, midway along the country's shoreline, is fairly steep and usually rocky. South of Beirut there are sandy stretches. The narrow coastal plain is characterized by warm summers, which provide ideal conditions for growing fruit. In this area early human civilizations cultivated grains and established communities. The same land is still used for farming; groves of orange and olive trees are a common sight, and bananas and grapes are also cultivated.

Lebanon is a strip of land 135 miles (217 km) long and only 20–55 miles (32–88 km) wide.

LEBANON MOUNTAINS Inland, the ground level rises quickly and meets the Lebanon Mountains, one of the country's two high mountain ranges. The Lebanon range follows the coastline from the northern border with Syria as far south as the mouth of the Litani River just north of Tyre. Wherever possible, terraces have been cut into the stone faces of the mountains and filled with soil to grow vegetables, with the lower slopes used for cultivating olives.

BEKÁA VALLEY The Bekáa Valley in the northern half of the country is the most fertile of Lebanon's regions, with the richest farmland in the country. It is Lebanon's main agricultural area. Tobacco, mulberries, potatoes, citrus fruits, and cotton are cultivated there, and aqueducts carry water from the Litani River to the crops.

ANTI-LEBANON RANGE The fourth geographical region is formed by the interior mountains known as the Anti-Lebanon range. These mountains run parallel to the Lebanon Mountains and straddle the eastern border with Syria. In the winter the mountains are characteristically frosty and snowcapped. Apart from scattered brush that grows when the weather is warm, there is little natural vegetation.

Lebanon in Arabic is Djebel Libnan, or "White-as-Milk Mountains," because the highest mountains in the country are covered with snow most of the year.

Many springs on the western slopes of the Lebanon Mountains form small rivers. Other rivers are seasonal, forming in the wet winters and drying up in the arid summers.

RIVERS

The Litani River, which is only 90 miles (145 km) long, is the country's longest and most important river. It starts just south of the city of Baalbek (also Baalbeck) and flows south between the two mountain ranges, turning west to meet the sea just north of Tyre. It was dammed in 1959, at the southern end of the Bekáa Valley, to form Lake Qaraaoun, providing water for irrigation. The Litani is the only river in the Near East that does not cross an international boundary.

The Orontes, Lebanon's other major river, flows north into Syria. Like the Litani, it irrigates agricultural land in the Bekáa Valley.

The Litani River runs through the Bekáa Valley.

MOUNT HERMON

The Arabic name for this mountain in the Anti-Lebanon range, straddling the border with Syria, translates as "Mountain of the Chief." It has three summits; the highest stands at 9,232 feet (2,814 m) above sea level.

For thousands of years the natural grandeur of Mount Hermon has inspired poets and religious mystics. The remains of a number of ancient temples have been found on its slopes, and it is believed to have been the site of the transfiguration of Jesus Christ.

The Orontes, which irrigates the Bekáa Valley, is called Nahr al-Asi, because it flows north through Syria and Turkey before draining into the Mediterranean.

CLIMATE

Lebanon's temperate climate—with some 300 sunny days a year—is a typically Mediterranean one, similar to that of southern California. Summers are hot and dry and winters warm and moist. The chief factor affecting the climate is altitude. Humidity is high along the coast, and Lebanese residents who can afford it move for part of the summer to a second home in the mountains, where the air is drier and cooler.

The mountains also serve as an important physical barrier. Rain-bearing clouds blowing in from the Mediterranean west of Lebanon release moisture when they reach the mountains. In the cool months from October through April, when rains fall in torrents along the coast, the mountains are capped in heavy snowfall. This ensures a supply of water later in the year when the snow melts.

The temperature in the summer months rarely exceeds 90°F (32°C) at sea level, while inland in the mountains the temperature is around 68°F (20°C) in the summer. In the winter the temperature on the coast averages 56°F (13°C). The Bekáa Valley is much drier and cooler than the rest of the country. As such, irrigation is necessary to ensure that there is enough water for the crops. While Beirut receives an average of 36 inches (91 cm) of rainfall each year, only 15 inches (38 cm) of rain falls in the Bekáa Valley.

FLORA

Common plants and trees include poppy, anemone, oak, fir, pine, and cypress. Along the coastal regions there are shrubs known as tamarisks, which can grow in soils with high levels of salt. The scaly leaves of the tamarisk grow on small twigs, giving the tree a feathery appearance. The stems of one particular species, *Tamarisk mannifera,* produce an edible honeylike substance that scale insects feed on. In spring, wildflowers, including the indigenous Lebanon violet, bloom on the hills and mountains.

"The trees of the Lord are watered abundantly, the cedars of Lebanon which he planted." This text from Psalms 104: 16-23 attests to the fame of the cedars in Lebanon. The tree, now a national symbol, grows to about 80 feet (24 m) in height.

CEDARS OF LEBANON The long-lived cedar, native to the eastern Mediterranean and other parts of Asia Minor, is an aromatic evergreen conifer with a very large trunk and a wide-spreading crown. Due to its reported ability to repel insects, the Phoenicians exported the tree to Egypt where, among other things, it was used for boats and coffins. In biblical times, Lebanon was renowned for its cedar forests, and King Solomon built his palace from the wood of Lebanese cedars. The tree was also considered medicinal—its pitch was used to ease toothaches.

Over the centuries the cedars have gradually been depleted. They once covered vast areas of the country but are now squeezed into an area of about 5,000 to 7,000 acres (2,000 to 2,800 ha), around 5 percent of the country's land area.

The most famous stand of cedars still surviving in Lebanon is at Bsharri in the Lebanon Mountains. The Barouk Cedars Nature Reserve and the Chouf Cedar Reserve are located in Chouf, a district under the Mount Lebanon governate. The oldest and largest specimens of the tree are reported to be over 2,000 years old. They are, unfortunately, in a very poor state and show little evidence of propagation. Mindless visitors make huge cuts on the bark and damage the trees, which are already suffering from receiving insufficient light and water due to overcrowding.

There are plans by environmental organizations to try to save the cedars of Lebanon by reforesting them in new and larger areas of the country. One example is the Chouf Cedar Reserve, situated southeast of Beirut. It is Lebanon's largest nature reserve, covering 123,550 acres (50,000 ha) of land and boasting six cedar forests. Although there are lesser cedar forests remaining in Lebanon, the tree is still the country's national emblem and is featured on the national flag.

A barrel of olives for sale in a market.

OLIVES　Olives are narrow-leaved evergreen trees that belong to a botanical family of over 30 different species. The common olive, *Olea europaea*, is native to the Mediterranean area and is grown in Lebanon wherever the climate allows. It is particularly common along the coast because the tree is suited to the dry summers and cool winters there. Both ripe and unripe olives have a very bitter taste, but the bitterness is removed by soaking them in an alkaline solution.

FAUNA

The most interesting animal found in Lebanon is the hyrax, a small mammal about the size of a domestic cat that looks like a guinea pig. It is classified by zoologists as a primitive ungulate (a hoofed mammal), distantly related to elephants. Its resemblance to the elephant can be seen only in its skeleton, its tusklike incisors, and certain features of its reproductive system.

A number of animals found in Lebanon are threatened with extinction. They include the gray wolf, the mountain gazelle, the imperial eagle, the Mediterranean monk seal, and a species of pelican.

Migratory birds such as cormorants, flamingos, herons, ducks, and pelicans visit the marshes of the Bekáa Valley on their way south in the fall and north in the spring. Birds native to Lebanon include songbirds like the thrush and nightingale.

The hyrax makes its home in rocky cliffs and feeds on tree leaves, grasses, and the young shoots of plants.

Boats docked at the port of Beirut's sheltered harbor.

CITIES

Lebanon's major cities lie along the coast, and many of them are ports either today or served as ports of call in historical times.

BEIRUT Lebanon is one of the most urbanized countries in the Arab world, with well over 1.57 million people living in this capital city and another 2.1 million in the surrounding metropolitan areas. Beirut alone is home to around 40 percent of the country's population. The city is located on the coastline, at the foot of the Lebanon Mountains.

Beirut has been an important commercial center since over a thousand years before Christ, despite its temporary disappearance for over a century after it was destroyed by a fire in 140 B.C. It has been rebuilt many times since, first by the Romans under Pompey and most recently in the 1990s after the civil war. It was first conquered by the Arabs in A.D. 635, and became a significant center of commerce under the Ottomans. The life story of the city mirrors Lebanon's history.

Beirut is a major seaport and handles the bulk of the country's imports and exports. The city has important rail, road, and air connections to other parts of the country as well as to other cities in the Middle East and Europe.

TRIPOLI Tripoli, the second most important city in Lebanon, is situated in the northwest of the country. Like Beirut, it is an important seaport.

Its port district is on a small peninsula some 2 miles (3 km) from the inland city center. Tripoli is also the terminal for a major oil pipeline from Iraq, and oil refining is a major industry there.

The city of Tripoli has an ancient heritage. Founded in 700 B.C. by the Phoenicians, it was taken by Muslims in A.D. 638 and held by them until 1109, when the Crusaders conquered and occupied the city. It has a famous old Frankish castle, Saint Giles. In 1289 the Egyptians destroyed the city, but it was later rebuilt. It became an important city under the Ottomans.

Today its major industries include olive harvesting and processing, soap manufacturing, tobacco cultivation, sugar refining, and sponge fishing.

The name Tripoli *has its roots in two Greek words:* tri, *meaning "three," and* poli, *"cities," because in ancient times it incorporated Tyre, Sidon, and Arados. Today the city consists of two parts: El Mina is the outlying peninsular port, while the main city is two miles inland.*

SPONGE FISHING

The sponges that occupied a place at most kitchen sinks before the invention of plastic sponges were the skeletons of a marine species found throughout the world. And if your kitchen or bath had one of the best quality sponges, it is possible the skeleton belonged to a marine animal scooped out of the Mediterranean Sea by a Lebanese fisherman.

Sponges are multicellular animals whose surface layer of cells covers an inner layer of flagellated cells (flagella are whiplike appendages) that move water through the animal, collecting food and providing a form of propulsion. There are numerous varieties of sponges throughout the world, but those found in the Mediterranean Sea are rated the best because of the softness of their skeletons.

Sponges are collected by fishermen who dive into the sea for them. The animal tissue is left in the sun to decompose; then the skeletal tissue, which does not decompose, is washed and bleached. Large sponges are cut into the familiar blocks that eventually find their way onto the shelves of specialty stores.

SIDON Another city with a castle dating back to the Crusades is Sidon (also known as Sayda), although the 13th century ruins are not the earliest reminder of Sidon's ancient heritage. Jesus Christ preached a sermon in Sidon on one of his journeys, and a number of important archaeological finds have been unearthed in the area. Phoenician burial sites, cut out of bare rock, have been found close to the city.

Sidon is situated in the southwest of the country. It is commercially important as a center for the export of olive oil and fruit. Known as the city of gardens since Persian times, Sidon today is still surrounded by citrus and banana plantations. Tobacco and figs, too, are cultivated in the surrounding countryside.

In the past, Sidon was known as a refuge which sheltered its fleet from storms and provided protection during military incursions.

TYRE Another ancient city is Tyre (also known as Soûr), and it is probably far older than Sidon. Tyre is said to have provided the 80,000 craftsmen who built King Solomon's palace in the 10th century B.C. The famous ancient Greek historian Herodotus traced the city's origins back to the 28th century B.C. This is consistent with Greek mythology, which recounts how a daughter of a king of Tyre captured the heart of Zeus. After falling in love, he escaped with her to a continent in the west that he named after his lover. Her name was Europa.

Tyre was the most important city in ancient Phoenicia. The Phoenicians extracted a highly valued dye from a shellfish, which became known as Tyrian purple. Cloth of this color was available only in this area at the time. Like Tripoli, Tyre was captured by Muslims in the seventh century. In the 12th century it was taken over by the Crusaders, who held it until 1291, when Muslim rule was reestablished. In 1982, as a result of a war between the Arabs and Israel, Tyre was badly damaged. With much of its central area surrounded by squatter settlements, Tyre today is still being rebuilt.

JBAIL Jbail (Jubayl or Jubay or Byblos, the ancient name), a small town some 22 miles (36 km) north of Beirut, is a serious contender for the claim of being the oldest town in the world. There are records of trade with Byblos in 2800 B.C., when the Egyptians arrived to barter for the papyrus they used for making a form of paper. It is said that the Greek word for book (*biblos*) thus the word "bible"—comes from the name of this town. Near Jbail are unique "wall tombs," shafts quarried into the rock as burial sites. Ancient Egyptian alabaster vases found in them give some idea of how old the tombs are.

Jbail is the site of the first Crusader castle built in the Levant, a name given to the countries along the eastern shores of the Mediterranean Sea.

OTHER CITIES Some cities have grown in importance only recently, while others have always been important as historical sites. Junia, once a village, is now a thriving port city just north of Beirut. The ancient city of Baalbek in the foothills of the Anti-Lebanon Mountains is famous for its Roman ruins; these include temples that were dedicated to Roman gods Jupiter and Bacchus. Zahlé (also Zahlah), which lies on the slopes of the Lebanon Mountains, is a resort whose popularity is evident by the numerous cafés doing brisk business on the banks of the Bardouni River.

Jbail, a famous harbor in historical times, is today a quiet fishing town.

17

HISTORY

IN THE PAST FEW YEARS Lebanon has been literally rebuilding itself, an ironic and tragic fact for a country that is steeped in thousands of years of history. Indeed, Lebanon's history accompanies some of the earliest and most important steps in the development of civilization.

EARLY TRADERS

The little that is known about the early inhabitants of the land now called Lebanon also applies to the entire Levant. This ancient region has rich alluvial soil, which would have attracted the Middle East's first farmers.

Rich land is also found in the Bekáa Valley, and there, too, early farmers settled down after migrating from Mesopotamia, home of the very early Sumerian and Babylonian civilizations. The excavation of a kiln-fired clay

Opposite: **The ruins of a Roman temple in Baalbek.**

Left: **The temple of Jupiter, which is located in Baalbek, stands in ruins — a far cry from its former glory.**

A king of Tyre and Sidon, Luli, fled from the Assyrians in the fleet of the Phoenician navy. The Phoenicians were early colonizers and traders, and their skill in navigation was well known.

sculpture dating back to 3000 B.C. is evidence of this. It is a figure of Astarte, also known as Ishtar, who was originally a Mesopotamian mother goddess of love and war. Other terra-cotta figures from around this period have also been found; nearly all are of nude female figures.

Finds of terra-cotta figures bearing elaborate hairstyles and jewelry show the influence of ancient Egyptian culture in the Levant. Pharaoh Ramses II (1304–1237 B.C.) passed through Lebanon in his war against the Hittites, whom he defeated in what is now Syria. The Obelisk Temple at Jbail clearly shows an Egyptian influence in its style and design.

In the ancient town of Byblos (Jbail), excavations have exposed town walls that date back to the Amorite period. "Amorite" is a general term for early groups of Semitic people who established communities in the Levant in Old Testament times. Amorite settlements along the coast were, naturally, engaged in local maritime trade and would also have traded with inland communities in what is now Syria and Jordan. Out of such a background there developed the first known commercial empire on earth, Phoenicia.

PHOENICIA

The word "Phoenicia" is said to be derived from a Greek word for purple, referring to the purple dye for which Tyre was famous. The city of Tyre was the Phoenician capital, seat of a commercial empire that

A THEORY ABOUT A DWARF-GOD WITH A BEARD

It is possible that the Phoenicians discovered America some 2,000 years before either the Vikings in the 10th century or the expedition 500 hundred years later led by Christopher Columbus. The evidence for putting forward this theory is partly based on the known seafaring prowess of the Phoenicians. They are believed to have sailed down the west coast of Africa and, in other expeditions, probably reached the southwest of Britain. Research has also revealed similarities between pre-Columbian American and Mediterranean civilizations. There are parallel examples in metallurgy, agriculture, mathematics, and language between Phoenician culture and those of the Olmecs and Mayas of the Americas.

One example given to support the claim of a cultural link is a dwarflike god, Bes, whose image adorned the prows of Phoenician ships. A "twin" dwarflike god has also been found in statues of the Olmec culture in Central America and of the Mayas of South America. What gives some weight to this example is that the American god is always shown with a beard, while in pre-Columbian American culture men did not grow beards. The bearded dwarf, it is claimed, crossed the Atlantic with his Phoenician admirers.

stretched westward to the Strait of Gibraltar and included the founding of Carthage, an ancient city-state, in the ninth century B.C. The Phoenicians traded linen, metal, glass, wood, ivory, and precious stones. Sometime around the eighth century B.C. the Phoenician cities came into conflict with Assyria, another ancient kingdom, and were weakened as a result. Subsequently, they fell under the influence of such other powerful groups as the Babylonians, the Persians, and, later, the Romans. As part of the Roman Empire, Lebanon was Christianized.

THE ROMANS

In 64 B.C. the Roman general Pompey the Great conquered Phoenicia after ridding the Mediterranean Sea of pirates. Using what is now Lebanon as a base, he went on to wage a successful war against the kings of Armenia and Syria. The whole region, including Jerusalem, became part of the Roman Empire.

The Romans wanted top-quality timber for their ships and buildings, and they found just what they needed in the forests of modern-day Lebanon. They kept guard over the forests and built roads to transport logs to the coast, from where they could be shipped to Rome.

By 1000 B.C. the Phoenicians had invented an alphabet that was the forerunner of several modern alphabets, including Arabic, Latin, and Hebrew. The ancient Greek historian Herodotus wrote that the Phoenicians were the first people to sail around Africa, which they may have done around 600 B.C.

The Romans are famous for the roads they built and carefully maintained. Roman milestones, recording the completion of road repairs, have been found in Lebanon.

MUSLIM RULE

The caliphs were religious and secular successors to Muhammad, the founder of Islam, and under the second caliph the first expansion of Islam outside of Arabia took place. In A.D. 630 the Arabs conquered Syria and annexed most of modern-day Lebanon, turning it into a military and political region governed from Damascus. A Damascus-based dynasty known as the Umayyads (oo-MY-ahdz) ruled until 750, when it was forcibly replaced by a rival caliphate. The new caliphs, the Abbasids (ah-BAH-sidz), established themselves in Baghdad.

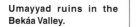

Umayyad ruins in the Bekáa Valley.

The Christians were allowed to practice their religion, but they were discriminated against and lost social and political power. In 759 and again in 760 there were revolts by Christian communities, but those rebellions were easily repressed.

As a result of the violent struggle between the Umayyads and the Abbasids, local dynasties emerged in Lebanon. A more centralized Muslim rule, however, was established again after the rise of the Mamluks, also known as Mamelukes, who overthrew the Abbasids in 1250.

THE CRUSADERS

Before the Crusaders arrived, the mountainous region of Lebanon known as Mount Lebanon was a refuge for persecuted minorities. The Christian Maronites settled there starting in the seventh century, and the Muslim Druze occupied the southern part of the mountains from the 11th century.

A Crusader castle in Jbail.

The majority of the Crusaders came from France, Germany, and Italy, with some from England. The Arabs called all of them Franks. The first Crusade expedition arrived in 1099 and the last one remained until the 14th century. The aim of the Crusades was to secure Christian rule over the Muslim-controlled holy places of the eastern Mediterranean, as Christian communities had been finding it increasingly difficult to withstand the growing influence of Islam in the country.

THE OTTOMANS

The Mamluk Muslim dynasties were still ruling Lebanon when, early in the 16th century, the Ottoman Turks arrived on the scene. The Ottomans conquered Lebanon and other regions of the eastern Mediterranean coast. Ottoman rule was based on economics, not religion, so they allowed non-Muslim communities to practice their own religions as long as they paid their taxes.

The more powerful local families were put in charge of collecting the taxes, and they became the base for influential dynasties that began to emerge in the late 16th and the 17th centuries. Descendants of some of these powerful families still dominate Lebanese politics. Two main dynasties controlled the political scene: the Maans and, later, the Shihabs. They formed alliances with various Muslim and Christian groups, chiefly

Deir el Kamar, an old Christian town in the mountains southeast of Beirut, was the Ottoman capital. Some buildings in this town were designed by Tuscan architects imported from Italy in the 17th century.

the Druzes and Maronites, but switching allegiances among the different power groups led to an instability in Lebanese politics that boded ill for the future.

Constant rivalry between Muslim and Christian groups took the form of religious conflicts, but they often disguised deeper economic inequalities among different groups of people. Increasing animosity between landlords and peasants and political differences between Druze and Maronite groups came to a head in 1858, and a fierce civil war raged for two years. It ended with an apparent victory for the Druze, but in 1859 foreign troops from European powers and the Ottoman Empire arrived in the country and established a new administration. This ensured that a Christian ruler governed the country, although Lebanon remained part of the Ottoman Empire. This arrangement lasted until World War I (1914–18).

FRENCH RULE

During World War I the Ottoman Empire supported Germany. After the war, three of the Allied powers (Britain, France, and Russia) divided the territories that had belonged to the vanquished, and the French emerged as the new rulers of Lebanon.

The French created the modern borders of Lebanon and established its identity as a separate country. Before that, the territory had always been part of larger provinces governed by empires based in Rome, Damascus, Medina, and Constantinople. The French brought together the Muslim coastal areas and the inland Christian mountain area into one administrative region.

In April 1920, Lebanon and Syria were placed under the French Mandate and General Henri Gouraud *(above)*.

The presence of various ethnic groups demanding greater political representation led to civil unrest after independence. A pro-Arab rebel group, some of whose members are seen above, was led by Kamal Jumblatt, a Lebanese politician.

Many Muslims were reluctant to accept their new identity as Lebanese because they saw the new country as being Western and Christian. The French and the Maronites supported one another, and when the country became independent in 1926, the Christians were left in a politically powerful position. The French had created one country but not a unified people. The basic conflict between Christian groups who looked to the West and Muslim groups who looked to the Arab world was an underlying cause of a civil war that would return Lebanon to the fractured conditions that existed before the French took over.

INDEPENDENCE

In 1926 the Lebanese republic was formed and a constitution was drawn up. The French were happy to accept this until 1943, when the Lebanese parliament declared independence. France imprisoned the president and the prime minister. To protest this action, there was a general strike and an uprising. Under pressure from Britain and the United States, France backed down.

As had often happened in history, the colonial power in Lebanon left behind a state of instability and conflict that it had largely created in the first place. A power-sharing system was set up in which government posts were divided between representatives of the main religious groups. A compromise was reached: the Christians renounced allegiance to the West, while the Muslims renounced union with Syria or other Arab states. The effect, however, was to institutionalize the differences between the religious groups, and because the Christians were given a disproportionate share of power, a bitter resentment arose among the increasing number of poor Shiite Muslims, also called Shia Muslims.

The powerful Christian lobby, meanwhile, began to express a wish to ally itself with the West and distance itself from the neighboring Arab world. Muslims naturally wished to have closer cooperation with other Arab states, and there were two coups, in 1949 and 1961, aimed at forming a union with Syria. In 1958 the first outbreak of war in Lebanon occurred when Lebanese people responded to the pan-Arab call of Egyptian president Gemal Abdel Nasser. The United States intervened for the first time in response to President Camille Chamoun's request for assistance against internal opposition and threats. By rendering support to the government, the United States successfully displaced opposing forces. The aftermath of the operation saw General Faud Chebab replacing Camille Chamoun as president.

In 1970 the Palestine Liberation Organization (PLO) moved its headquarters to Lebanon after being expelled from Jordan. As the Arab-

ISRAEL INVADES

In 1978 Israel invaded the southern part of Lebanon, primarily to repel the Palestinian rebels and secondarily to support a particular Christian faction, the South Lebanon Army. Israel invaded again in 1982; the assassination of the Christian president-elect, Bashir Gemayel, in 1982 brought an Israeli advance of armed forces to Beirut, and the city was kept under siege for three months. The PLO was seriously threatened by the Israelis and was forced to withdraw from Beirut, relocating to Tunis under protection from an international army.

When West Beirut was occupied by the Israeli army, a massacre of Palestinians by Christian militias took place in the Sabra and Shatila refugee camps. This bloodshed led to the deployment of United Nations peacekeeping forces. The Israeli invasion left 12,000 Lebanese and Palestinians dead, 40,000 wounded, 300,000 homeless, and 100,000 without shelter.

Every year, Lebanese Christians gather together to remember their fellow comrades who were killed during Lebanon's 1975-1990 civil war.

Israeli conflict deepened, Palestinians expelled from Israel sought refuge in Lebanon, where other Palestinians had fled when the state of Israel was created in 1948. By 1975 Palestinians in Lebanon numbered more than 300,000. Raids were organized across the border into the Jewish state, adding to the tensions that were beginning to tear Lebanon apart.

CIVIL WAR

In 1975 fighting erupted between Muslim and Christian factions. It began when shots were fired into a church congregation where the Christian president was worshipping. The car used in the attack was identified as belonging to a Palestinian group. A few hours later a bus carrying Palestinians was fired on by Christian soldiers, and 27 were left dead. A civil war had begun. In the following year, the PLO joined forces with the Muslims.

In 1983 terrorist bombs killed more than 300 American and French troops, and Western forces eventually pulled out of Lebanon. This allowed civil conflict to break out once more. Westerners in Beirut became the target of Muslim kidnappers in 1984, and in 1987 Syrian troops occupied Beirut. In the south of the country the Israeli army continued to battle with Palestinian troops. Beirut became a city divided: East Beirut was Christian, West Beirut was Muslim. The demarcation line between the two became known as the Green Line, and this border was often the scene of fierce fighting. The country was governed by a bewildering array of militias, each of which controlled its own territory.

Over the next two years Lebanon teetered on the brink of collapse. The rival Muslim and Christian groups could not agree on whom should be president.

PEACE AT LAST—ALMOST

Toward the end of 1989 negotiations between the rival power groups led to a new constitution that gave increased power to Muslims. With Syrian support the Taif Agreement, a framework for national reconciliation named after the place in Saudi Arabia where the leaders met, was brought into effect. In 1991 nearly all of the Western hostages were released. The Green Line dividing Beirut was dismantled, and young people were able to visit the other side of their capital for the first time.

A man removes rubble from what was fomerly known as the Beirut Green Line.

In 1992 voting for a new National Assembly took place for the first time in 20 years—17 years after the first incidents that had led to the civil war. The elected prime minister, Rafiq al-Hariri, set about rebuilding war-ravaged Beirut.

The end of the civil war found most militias weakened or disbanded. Palestinian troops that used to occupy southern Lebanon as a base for attacking Israel withdrew in May 2000. The assassination of Rafiq al-Hariri in 2005 triggered the Cedar Revolution, in which Lebanese groups began to demand that Syria withdraw its 15,000-strong army forces as well as end its interference in Lebanese affairs. In April 2005 Syria finally withdrew from Lebanon. Lebanon is slowly moving toward a sense of normality and stability.

GOVERNMENT

IN OCTOBER 1990, WHEN THE CIVIL WAR ENDED, Lebanon began to rebuild its political institutions. The most important change was that Muslims would have a greater say in the running of their country than before. After the end of the French mandate in 1943, political control of the country had always been in the hands of a Christian presidency. After the civil war, political authority was in the hands of a Muslim prime minister and there was a more equitable Christian-Muslim representation in the 128 deputy parliament.

Above: **Lebanese political party members meeting in parliament.**

Opposite: **A government building in Beirut.**

THE CONSTITUTION

Although Lebanon became independent in 1943, the constitution (which has been amended several times) dates from 1926. Lebanon is a republic, with universal suffrage, which means that every adult citizen age 21 and over has the right to vote.

The formal head of government is the prime minister, who is chosen by the president in consultation with the 128 members of the National Assembly. Elections to the National Assembly normally take place every four years. The last election was held in 2005. The National Assembly at that time was made up of the Rafiq Hariri Martyr List with 72 seats, the Resistance and Development Bloc with 35 seats, and the Aoun Alliance with 21 seats. By custom, the president is a Maronite Christian, the prime minister is a Sunni Muslim, and the speaker of the National Assembly is a Shiite Muslim. This tripartite division based on religion dates back to 1943 when the country first achieved independence. At that time an agreement was made that all government bodies would be proportioned

The six governorates (administrative regions) in Lebanon are Beirut, Mount Lebanon, Bekáa, North Lebanon, Nabatiyeh, and South Lebanon.

on the basis of six Christians to five Muslims. This division was always unfair because Christians did not make up a majority of the population. It gave undue power to the Christians and caused resentment and conflict. This eventually led to the civil war that ended with a new constitution, formalized in 1990 following the Taif Agreement, giving Muslims their proper majority voice in the running of the country.

HIZBOLLAH

Hizbollah (also known as Hezbollah) is a radical Shiite Muslim organization. It has its roots in the poorest minority of Arabs living in Lebanon. These Arabs were politicized by the impact of Israel's invasions in 1978 and 1982, and Hizbollah, or the Party of God, was the name given to their political organization. The growth of Hizbollah has been funded by large amounts of money from Iran.

A portrait of Hizbollah General Secretary Hassan Nasrallah in Beirut, the capital of Lebanon.

MR. MIRACLE

Rafiq al-Hariri, who became Lebanon's prime minister after the end of the civil war and held the post until his resignation in 2004, was nicknamed Mr. Miracle by Lebanese newspapers. He was an extremely rich man and was recognized as one of the world's 100 wealthiest people. As prime minister, he had set himself the task of spearheading the rebuilding of his country and played an important role in jumpstarting Lebanon's international investment and economic revival. He put $100 million into an investment project for the rebuilding of Beirut, and, since 1982, he paid university fees for 30,000 Lebanese studying at home and abroad.

It has been said that he would indeed have to be a Mr. Miracle to survive as Lebanon's leading politician. Many political leaders have been assassinated by rival groups, and Rafiq al-Hariri required massive security to thwart the attempts on his life. He personally employed 40 private bodyguards and drove in a convoy of six armored Mercedes accompanied by armed soldiers in other vehicles. The central government offices were equipped with blast-resistant armor plating and bulletproof glass. In spite of these precautions, al-Hariri was assassinated on February 14, 2005, by explosives when his convoy was in Beirut. His assassination remains under investigation, and suspected Syrian officials, with whom al-Hariri had an uneasy relationship, have been asked to extend their cooperation in the matter. In June 2005 the Beirut International Airport was renamed Beirut Rafiq Hariri International Airport in his honor.

Hizbollah is engaged in both peaceful politics and armed conflicts. It has representatives in the new political system, and it has increased its political clout by gaining 14 seats in the Lebanese cabinet. Its funding from Iran allows it to develop and maintain an extensive social welfare program for the poorest sections of Lebanese society. Much needed hospitals, schools, and food stores are run by Hizbollah, and it gives assistance that the central government is not yet able to provide. Hizbollah also has an influential TV station called al-Manar (The Lighthouse).

After Israel's withdrawal from south Lebanon in 2000 and the retreat of Syrian troops in 2005, Hizbollah became the most powerful military force in Lebanon. It is currently under pressure to demilitarize and integrate its forces into the Lebanese army. Hizbollah has yet to do so as the current border tension with Israel regarding the Shebaa Farms area has not been resolved. It is likely, however, that once Israel pulls out of the contested area, Hizbollah would have little choice but to hand in its weapons and merge into the Lebanese army.

In November 2006, Lebanese cabinet minister Pierre Gemaye—a Christian and a key member of the anti-Syrian majority in the Lebanese parliament—was shot dead in an assassination that raised tensions between opponents and allies of Syria.

THE LEBANESE ARMED FORCES

Some of the Lebanese Armed Forces's (LAF) primary missions are maintaining security and stability in the country, guarding the country's borders and ports, relief and rescue operations, firefighting, and combating drug trafficking. The army, air force, and navy make up the three branches of the LAF, and they are operated and coordinated by the LAF Command in Yarzeh, east of Beirut. Lebanon has six military colleges and schools. Promising cadets may be sent to other countries to receive further training.

Beside the commando and artillery regiments, the Lebanese army is also made up of the Republican Guard Brigade, which is responsible for protecting the president by traveling with him.

The air force currently lacks operational capability. The few fighter pilot aircraft it owns are old and of no use in combat. Lebanon does invest in active aircraft like helicopters, however, that are used on a variety of domestic missions, mainly in battling narcotics trafficking and other violations.

The Lebanese navy, on the other hand, is very active. It is charged with protecting Lebanon's waters and ports and for keeping watch over illegal smuggling of goods.

Previously Lebanon had mandatory military service of one year for men. In May 2005 the new conscription system reduced compulsory service to only a six-month period. The new system also pledged to phase out all conscription in two years.

A photograph of Lebanon's former prime minister, the late Rafiq al-Hariri.

34

BORDER TENSION

Although Israel withdrew from Lebanon in May 2000, 19 square miles (49 square km) of heavily contested land—referred to as Shebaa Farms, on the northwestern slope of Mount Hermon, at the junction of Lebanon, Syria and Israel—is still under Israel's control. The issue is nebulous as to whether this area belongs to Lebanon or to the part of Syria known as the Golan Heights, which was occupied by Israel from 1967 to 2000. Syria's refusal to clearly demarcate the border has made the situation tense, although Syria has verbally agreed that the area belongs to Lebanon.

This is largely the reason for Hizbollah's continued hostilities toward Israel, resulting in tensions and cross-border attacks. In November 2005 Hizbollah launched an ambush along the entire border with Israel in a bid to abduct Israeli troops in the village of Al-Ghajar.

Another attack was launched in December 2005 when rockets were fired from Hizbollah territory into the Israeli village of Kiryat Shmona. The UN Security Council condemned Hizbollah for inciting hostilities and called on the Lebanese government to put an end to such attacks.

In retaliation, Israel sabotaged the runways and refueling tanks of Beirut's international airport. It also attacked on the seafront, creating a full naval blockade of Lebanon and turning away oil tankers and other vessels approaching Lebanese waters. Many bridges in southern Lebanon were also destroyed.

Hizbollah responded by launching over 100 rockets into northern Israel that reached as far south as Haifa. The UN Interim Force in Lebanon (UNIFIL), charged with maintaining peace, obtained a ceasefire, but the situation remained tense.

Lebanese prime minister Fouad Siniora called on the international community to pressure Israel to move out of the Shebaa Farms area.

The United States Agency for International Developments (USAID) deploys a truckload of humanitarian aid for Lebanon.

The Israel-Lebanon 2006 conflict killed over 1,500 Lebanese civilians and displaced about 1 million others.

Hizbollah seconded this opinion, claiming that the Israeli attacks were a violation of Lebanese sovereignty.

On July 12, 2006, another Israel-Lebanon border tension broke out when Hizbollah fired multiple rockets at Israeli military bases and border villages. This was in actual fact a diversionary tactic that was staged to capture two Israeli soldiers as hostages for the exchange of Arab prisoners in Israeli jails. Israel retaliated with air strikes and artillery attacks, and by imposing an air and naval blockade as well as launching a major ground invasion of southern Lebanon. In the wake of the Israeli attacks, some 130,000 homes, 350 schools, and 2 hospitals were destroyed. Numerous sewage plants and 400 miles (644 km) of road were also damaged. It was estimated that the damage done to Lebanese infrastructure amounts to a staggering $7 billion to $10 billion. About a month later the United Nations passed a resolution to end the conflict, calling for Israel's withdrawal, the disarming of Hizbollah, and the deployment of Lebanese soldiers in southern Lebanon. Both Israel and Lebanon agreed to the cessation of retaliatory attacks. As part of the UN proposal, the number of the United Nations Interim Forces in Lebanon (UNIFIL) was increased in southern Lebanon to restore and maintain the peace.

HUMAN RIGHTS AND JUSTICE

After so many years of civil war it is not surprising that human rights have suffered. The law does require a suspect to be released after 48 hours unless charges are made, but this is not always followed in practice. People on trial do have the right to a lawyer, but only if they can afford to pay for one. This means, of course, that poor people are at a serious disadvantage in the courtroom, since the system does not provide for legal aid.

There are a number of different courts. Besides the regular civilian court there is also a military court, which handles all cases involving members of military groups. There are also religious tribunals for the various Muslim and Christian denominations. These handle disputes involving marriage and inheritance.

In the refugee camps, Palestinian groups operate their courts, and Hizbollah and the Islamic militia conduct theirs in a similar manner. In the cases heard in the camps, Islamic law is applied to them, causing occasional conflicts with the laws of Lebanon.

Refugees in a Palestinian camp are governed by Islamic laws.

37

ECONOMY

LEBANON IS MAKING A BRAVE ATTEMPT to rise above the economic chaos created by the long years of civil war. In the process of restructuring its economy, it is showing the world that it does have a future as a nation. Throughout the 1980s Lebanon was written off as a nation, and there were predictions that the country would break up into an unstable number of mini states. This has not happened, and Lebanon is busily building a new economy as a nation state.

PRE–CIVIL WAR ECONOMY

Before 1975 Lebanon ranked as one of the 35 upper-middle-income countries of the world. The country's economy was anchored in trade, and two-thirds of the national income came from trade, banking, and tourism. Foreign visitors were attracted to the combination of a pleasant climate and a wealth of historical remains. This kind of economy depends on stability. Not surprisingly, the civil war destroyed the economy. Tourists and investors do not want to risk their lives or money in a country at war with itself.

Another problem was caused by the loss of central government control. A number of regions were controlled by local militias. The central government was unable to collect taxes in those areas, so the years of factional fighting seriously damaged Lebanon's economy. This results in rising unemployment and a very high rate of inflation, serious problems for those who are poor to begin with. As a result, the poor get poorer and the rich get richer.

Above: **The desolation of Martyr's Place in Beirut is a reminder of the civil war, but a clear sign that tourism is returning to Lebanon is this boy selling paintings of Martyr's Place before the war.**

Opposite: **The signs of rebuilding and construction in the city of Beirut.**

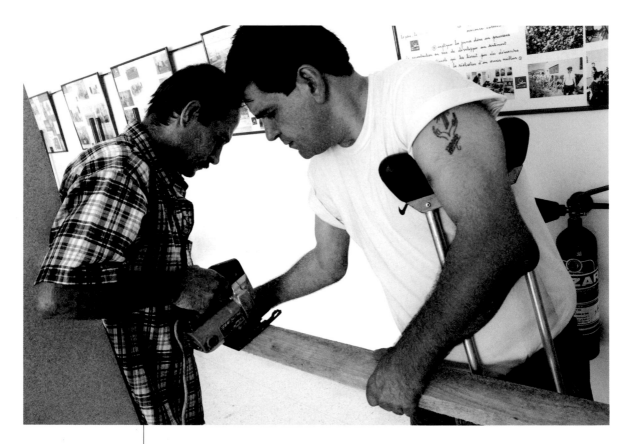

Lebanese men commonly take on jobs that require hard labor, such as construction.

COUNTRY IN TRANSITION

Lebanon is still trying to find its bearings economically, although it has been more than a decade since the civil war. Its economic outlook is recovering and looking positive despite its mounting debts. From 1992 to 1998 annual inflation fell more than 100 percent to 5 percent, and foreign exchange reserves also saw improvements in a rise to more than $6 billion from a previous $1.4 billion. Two of the factors for Lebanon's economic recovery are a sound banking system and international aid.

The rapidly increasing population has put a strain on the government, however, especially since a reasonable standard of health care and education is mainly restricted to those who can afford to pay for it. The backlash for the lack of educated youths is that poorer young people may become socially and economically displaced adults in the context of Lebanon's development.

HORIZON 2000

Horizon 2000 is the name of the government's master plan to rebuild Lebanon. The plan was first announced in 1993, about 18 months after the last shell of the civil war destroyed yet one more building in old Beirut. The goal is to restore Beirut to its pre-1975 status as a major international business and banking center.

By the end of the civil war the country's infrastructure was in a state of serious disrepair. Only one in three of the country's telephones were working, and electricity was restricted to six hours a day in Beirut. Outside the capital, electricity was nonexistent in many places. Water was also in short supply, and when it was available, it was often polluted.

Rebuilding Beirut is a massive task that begins with demolishing bombed-out buildings and removing the rubble.

The total cost of Horizon 2000 was initially estimated at $13 billion, but spiraling costs has put the final figure at $20 billion. This presents a major problem to Lebanon because the country is presently making only about $4.9 billion a year, while its total expenditure is at approximately $6.6 billion. Therefore, it is not surprising that Lebanon's public debt is an estimated 170 percent of its gross domestic product (GDP). This means that aid is now required from international donors for loans at lower than usual interest rates.

The plan to rebuild the city center of Beirut is a controversial one, primarily because of the cost. The city's central area was previously the zone that bridged the east and west sides of the divided city during the civil war.

So many buildings had been damaged that well over half of the area had to be demolished and cleared away before rebuilding could begin.

Construction workers on a high-rise building in Beirut.

It is estimated that some $30 billion was deposited abroad by Lebanese citizens during the civil war. It is hoped that, as confidence returns, most of these funds will flow back into the country's economy.

Although Beirut is now largely reconstructed, the huge debt that the Lebanese government accumulated has negative implications for its national economy and the Lebanese people. Critics say this unnecessary zeal to redo Beirut has led to neglect of need to restore decent living conditions for ordinary citizens in other parts of the country.

MAKING A CHOICE

Lebanon faces many challenges as it tries to recreate a viable economy that will provide work for its citizens. The major challenge is to find the huge amount of money needed to get various projects off the ground. The government of Lebanon has decided to use private capital as well as foreign aid for most of the important rebuilding and restructuring programs.

A good example of the government's approach was its program to rebuild Beirut. One aspect of that was dealing with the large number of owners and tenants who had claims on the land and buildings. An estimated 50,000 people had claims, and they were all affected by a law the government had passed to deal with this situation. Under that law, property owners could choose to sell their land to a company that was set up to manage the entire rebuilding project. The only alternative was to reclaim their land and themselves carry out all necessary reconstruction within a fixed period of time.

Some people say this was unfair because owners without sufficient funds had little choice but to sell their land to the company. The large profits expected to flow from the new Beirut city center will never be shared with the original owners of the buildings and land. Instead, private investors have been invited to buy shares in the project. Many of these investors are foreign companies, and they have effectively acquired property that once belonged to Lebanese citizens. Analysts of this policy point out that it is typical of a government more interested in creating profits for private companies than in developing an economic climate wherein all Lebanese will share in the hoped-for prosperity. The gap between the small number of rich people and the mass of poor people is said to be widening as a result.

A couple of mechanics repair a damaged car in front of their workshop in Beirut.

NATURAL RESOURCES

Lebanon is not rich in mineral resources. Its land, however, is very good for cultivation because of its rich alluvial soil. Limestone is abundant and is quarried extensively. Other minerals such as iron ore and salt are also found there.

The country's fast-flowing rivers, especially the Litani, are being developed for hydroelectric power and for the irrigation of the surrounding agricultural land. So far there have been three hydroelectric plants built on the Litani, with the one in Bekáa Valley being Lebanon's largest power facility.

AGRICULTURE

Approximately one-third of Lebanese land is arable. The typical agricultural use of land in the country involves cutting terraces into mountain slopes, as is the case in the Bekáa Valley, where land is the most fertile. Over 1,189 square miles (3,080 square km) of land area is used for agriculture, mainly grain cultivation. Typical farms in the Bekáa Valley are small, just over 7 acres (less than 3 ha).

Important farm products are grains, citrus fruit, figs, grapes, mulberries, apples, and bananas. Tomatoes, potatoes, and olives are also found on most farms. Between the years 2000 to 2005, agriculture contributed approximately 7.4 percent to Lebanon's GDP.

A harvester bites off a piece of squash to demonstrate how tasty it is.

The long dry summer months cause a shortage of water for farmers who, over the centuries, have fine-tuned all available means of irrigation. One ambitious attempt to channel water to where it is most needed is the Bekáa Irrigation Project, which involves harnessing the country's longest river, the Litani. So far the project has successfully irrigated 4,942 acres (2,000 ha) of land close to Beirut. The next phase would be to irrigate a further 16,556 acres (6,700 ha) of land.

NARCOTICS

Lebanon has been a major player in the production and distribution of narcotics, primarily opium and hashish. Both poppy and cannabis, or hemp, from which opium and marijuana respectively are derived, are cultivated in the Bekáa Valley. Both drugs are also smuggled into Lebanon for processing, before being smuggled out again to the United States and Europe. Lebanon's traditional banking secrecy laws are believed to help illegal organizations involved in money-laundering operations arising from drugs.

In recent years the government has attempted to eradicate the illicit drug trade. The ultimate success of this, however, depends on convincing farmers to switch to the cultivation of staple crops such as plums and wheat, which are far less lucrative. This is not easy to achieve, as the sale of narcotics, when it was at its peak in 1988, brought in a staggering $1.5 billion to Lebanon. The United Nations has promised to fund irrigation projects and to give alternative crop subsidies and other incentives to compensate farmers for the substitution of crops.

In the late 1980s about 39,537 acres (16,000 ha) of land was used for cannabis cultivation, yielding as much as 1,000 tons of cannabis resin. With the ongoing crackdown against the cultivation of narcotics, in 2002 it was estimated that the country reduced the cultivation of cannabis to 6,178 acres (2,500 ha). Opium poppy cultivation has also dropped by more than half.

Another ambitious endeavor is the Litani Water Project, which will cost $460 million to implement. Once completed, it will benefit 99 villages and thousands of acres of agricultural land in the south. With loans from Kuwait and the Arab Development Fund, it is likely that the first phase will be completed in 2007. The second phase will focus on a series of 22 irrigation networks that will provide water to 37,065 acres (15,000 ha) of land in the south.

INDUSTRY

The country is gradually reestablishing the industries that gave regular employment before the interruptions caused by the civil war. The main industries are banking, tourism, food processing, chemicals, oil refining, cement, furniture, and textiles. Most industrial enterprises are small scale and privately owned, and are concentrated around Beirut. The government, in a bid to promote investment and growth in the industry, has provided such fiscal incentives as reduced customs duties and tax exemptions for the industrial facilities in Lebanon.

CONSTRUCTION

Before the civil war, Lebanon had enjoyed a rapidly increasing urban population that pushed the demand for increased housing in Beirut. Postwar Lebanon also encountered a construction boom when the government began to repair damaged buildings in downtown Beirut. As a result, real estate prices for prime property skyrocketed. The boom was also fueled by the combined funds of local, expatriate, and Persian Gulf Arab investors, who see land and construction as attractive investment opportunities.

Lebanon also hosts "Project Lebanon," an international trade fair for construction technology, materials, and equipment. This yearly affair serves as a platform for potential investors from international companies to showcase their products and services and also to explore opportunities for themselves in the building and construction sector in Lebanon.

TOURISM

Lebanon's natural beauty, mild climate, historic legacy, and its strategic proximity to the Mediterranean Sea have made it a popular choice for tourists. Prior to the civil war, tourists contributed approximately 20 percent to Lebanon's GDP. After the war it proved to be difficult to attract visitors. In the first 11 months of 2004, however, there was a record 1.2 million tourists traveling to Lebanon, whereas in past years tourists averaged only around 300,000. This increase is due to the many wealthy Saudis and other Gulf Arabic tourists who chose not to holiday in the United States after the September 11, 2001, terrorist attacks.

In 2005 the assassination of Lebanon's former prime minister Rafiq al-Hariri raised some doubts as to whether Lebanon is truly the safest country in the Middle East. Although Lebanon has garnered $1 billion of direct foreign investment to revive its tourism industry, should there be any hint of a civil war recurrence, Lebanon will find it even harder to rebuild itself and regain the trust of investors and visitors.

IMPORTS AND EXPORTS

Due to its lack of natural resources, Lebanon has always had to import far more than it exports. Consumer goods account for a large share of the imports, along with cars, livestock, clothing, medicinal products, tobacco, machinery, transport equipment, and petroleum products.

Despite its trade imbalance, prior to the civil war Lebanon was not in danger of falling into increasing debt. It had been able to earn vast sums of money from what economists call invisible earnings. Tourists visiting the country spent their foreign currencies, and this was a major source of invisible earnings. Even more profitable was income earned through financial dealings involving banking and insurance. The country is now trying to rebuild these industries.

The main exports are agricultural products, chemicals, precious and semiprecious metals, construction minerals, electric power machinery, paper, and jewelry. The principal countries that trade with Lebanon are neighboring Middle East states, France, Germany, Switzerland, Italy, China, the United Kingdom, and the United States.

BANKING CAPITAL OF THE MIDDLE EAST?

Before civil war began in 1975, Beirut held the undisputed claim of being the banking capital of the Middle East. The present mission is to reestablish this claim within the next few years. It is not an unrealistic aim, partly because in the interim no other city in the Middle East was able to even approach the status that Beirut had once commanded.

Part of Beirut's success as a trusted financial center lay in its banking secrecy laws. Beirut and Zurich were equally renowned when it came to offering investors the highest degree of security, privacy, and protection. At a time when most of the Middle East, unlike Western Europe, suffered from an "image problem" in terms of internal stability, the financial institutions based in Beirut were able to offer a haven of international security and trust. Beirut's banks attracted billions of investors' dollars from neighboring countries and overseas. As a result, over one-quarter of Lebanon's national income was based on services to non-Lebanese.

There are positive signs that Beirut will be able to rebuild its image as the Arab capitalist powerhouse. Some of the millions of dollars that flowed out of the country after 1975 are trickling back into secret bank accounts. In 1999, $33.9 billion was deposited into Lebanese commercial banks, an amazing increase from the total deposits of $6.5 billion in 1992.

To further establish Beirut as a regional financial services center, the Central Bank has set up a central depositary, settlement, and clearing agency. The famous Casino du Libyan, once an icon of Beirut's status as the social and business hub of the Arab world, reopened in 1996 after being rebuilt. A sure sign that Beirut is recapturing international trust and recognition is the fact that familiar American fast-food chains have opened branches in the city.

Many factors that generated Beirut's image as the successful capitalist center of the Middle East are still there. In particular, work on the reconstruction of the Duty Free Zone has been completed at the port of Beirut, which was once the most important port in the eastern Mediterranean. Another project is to expand the rebuilt port in a bid to regain its dominant role as the conduit for trade involving countries such as Syria, Iraq, and Iran.

Beirut remains the financial center of Lebanon, while other coastal cities play greater roles than ever before as shipping hubs. The port of Sidon, or Sayda, is also an important terminal for oil refining.

ENVIRONMENT

LEBANON'S ENVIRONMENT HAD SUFFERED much abuse even before the long civil war. Deforestation had been practiced many times, from the pharaohs of ancient Egypt, who used cedar wood in the construction of their pyramids and palaces, to the Romans and to the Turks. Currently, problems like air pollution, illegal quarrying, and inadequate infrastructure for the treatment of waste have all further aggravated Lebanon's already frail environment.

More than a decade of neglect during the war has resulted in the lack of enforcement of environmental regulations, and conservation efforts have been largely nonexistent. After the war, government effort was concentrated mainly on rebuilding the country's basic infrastructure, and environmental concerns were neglected. It has taken Lebanon a long time to realize the severity of their environmental woes, but now it is taking small steps to preserve and conserve what little remains of its natural beauty.

Above: **An aerial view of Beirut reveals the amount of smog that is generated by the city's airborne pollutants.**

Opposite: **Cleaning up one of Lebanon's rivers as an environmental project.**

AIR POLLUTION

The growing number of people living and working in the city of Beirut has given rise to serious environmental problems. The lack of a functional public transportation system begets an excessive number of private cars belching out noxious exhaust fumes. Lebanon has one of the highest automobile densities in the world. Some 60 percent of privately owned vehicles in the country are in Greater Beirut. Gasoline sold in Lebanon has high levels of lead, thus rendering air pollution in the city to be among the highest in the world.

There is also a lack of proper research on air pollution. A promise by the government to implement a European Union–funded project to measure the levels of air pollution throughout Beirut and its suburbs has yet to be realized. In 2004 the number of public buses dropped from 200 to less than 100, further promoting the use of private transportation and exacerbating air pollution.

Although the Lebanese government passed Environmental Law 341 for the purpose of reducing air pollution and encouraging the use of less polluting fuels, this law has yet to be enforced.

LAND WOES

SAND AND GRAVEL QUARRYING The ambitious postwar rebuilding of Lebanon requires massive amounts of quarry by-products such as sand and rocks. Quarrying destroys much of Lebanon's natural vegetation and disrupts Lebanon's wildlife habitats. Quarrying also reduces the aesthetic quality of its surroundings and affects the health of animals and humans alike through dust and other air pollutants. There are more than 700 quarries in Lebanon, and more than half are in Mount Lebanon province, of which many are abandoned. A ban on quarrying was proclaimed in 2003.

A thousand tons of stone lies in Bekáa Valley, probably abandoned due to illegal quarrying.

Unfortunately, illegal quarrying persisted. The future of the activity remains uncertain because exceptions to the ban are handed out to quarry owners and the procedures for licensing are unclear.

AGRICULTURAL DEGRADATION Lebanese farmers not only practice excessive use of pesticides and fertilizers, they also do not adhere to the necessary waiting period between spraying and harvesting to ensure that their agricultural products are safe for consumption. Soil quality is therefore compromised, and the resulting runoff from the use of agricultural pesticides pollutes Lebanon's groundwater.

There is a need for the Ministry of Agriculture to reach and advise farmers on correct agricultural practices. There are campaigns underway, however, to promote awareness of the dangers of pesticide overuse. Over the past 20 years the total use of fertilizers has decreased as farmers have learned alternatives to chemical pesticides and fertilizers. Voluntary organizations have also taken it upon themselves to monitor the safe and effective use of agrochemicals.

POLLUTED WATERS

SEWAGE The Mediterranean Sea, which once provided attractive beaches for vacationers, has degenerated and been polluted to an unhealthy degree. Over the years garbage and sewage have been dumped into the sea by all the countries around the Mediterranean. According to environmentalists, during the years of conflict, militias accepted toxic waste from Europe in exchange for money. The waste was then dumped into the deep sea or coastal waters. In Sidon the coastline is dotted with open dumps, and toxic solid wastes are discarded straight into the sea without prior decontamination.

As a result, the surface water is often covered with small particles of raw sewage, which sometimes gather into ugly masses of yellow muck. The few patches of unpolluted beach near Beirut that have survived are now the domain of private resorts, which charge for admission.

UNPLANNED CONSTRUCTION OF BUILDINGS
Highly accelerated projects are being launched almost everywhere along the coast, particularly in north Beirut. There are few government controls. There was difficulty enforcing building regulations during the civil war, and little or no control over where and how buildings were constructed. As a result, they were often built too close to one another, with little or no provision for sewage treatment. The lack of proper infrastructure for waste disposal poses health risks and attracts infectious disease–carrying rodents, flies, and insects.

SHELLING The shelling of villages and towns during the civil war resulted in the pollution of the water table and most of the natural springs. People had little choice but to dig makeshift wells, and those, too, soon became polluted. People living in the refugee camps in Beirut have had to learn to cope with inadequate sewage facilities and unsafe drinking water. A 2001 UNICEF report estimated that 260 children in Lebanon die each year from diseases associated with the lack of potable water and with inadequate sanitation and hygiene.

The Lebanese government is working on building several water treatment plants in such areas as Sidon, Beirut, Tripoli, and Zahlé. To improve the standard of drinking water, the Ministry of Environment decreed that drinking water is to be treated with chlorine. Meanwhile, many industries continue to pollute underground aquifers, waterways, valleys, and coastal areas by unrestricted dumping.

Greenpeace activists investigating the source of polluted water in Lebanon.

A cedar reforestation reserve in Lebanon.

CONSERVATION EFFORTS

The cost of environmental degradation in Lebanon is estimated to be $565 million a year or 3.4 percent of its GDP. This affects the country economically, politically, and socially. Because of weak state control in the implementation of environmental measures, and the lack of a better standard of living, the population suffers from the burdens of diseases and premature death.

It is therefore encouraging that Lebanon recognizes the value of conservation. This is seen most clearly in the establishment of a Ministry of Environment in 1993 and in the growing number of environmentalist groups like Green Line, a voluntary organization promoting awareness and conservation of the environment.

Since 1992, Lebanon has declared 8 nature reserves, 12 forests, and several river basins and mountains as being protected areas. In addition,

NATURE PARKS AND RESERVES

The government, volunteer organizations, and private entrepreneurs have made much effort to conserve and protect what remains of Lebanon's trees and wildlife. Funding from various local and international private organizations, as well as the government, has made it possible to run these nature reserves. The Ministry of the Environment is the guardian of Lebanon's nature reserves.

the Green Plan Project was initiated to control soil erosion and to prohibit animals, particularly goats and sheep, from grazing on protected areas. The Ministry of Agriculture has joined in these efforts. It has banned tree logging and can punish violators with a fine and a jail term.

Although little was done to encourage waste reduction, efforts have been directed into recycling. A community waste and collection program by the Center for the Environment and Development was established, teaching the public how to convert used items into useful products. Schools have also initiated recycling campaigns. Between 1995 and 1997, 75,000 tons of paper were collected and recycled. Suckles, a private waste management company, has placed containers for glass, plastic, and metal around Beirut, where residents can sort their waste for recycling. In Lebanon there are at least five companies that recycle paper, four for glass and a few others for recycling metal and plastic. The Ministry of Environment is also investigating ways to reduce Lebanon's dependency on plastic shopping bags.

Promoting Lebanon as an ecological destination for hikers not only promotes tourism but also helps disseminate information on Lebanon's environmental concerns. Such an increase in environmental awareness bodes well for the nation's fragile environment.

ECOLOGY TREATIES

Environmental preservation is a hard-fought battle in Lebanon. The state is not always willing to put environmental needs above economic ones. Nevertheless, Lebanon has signed and ratified the International Convention for Desertification on rehabilitating the country's forested areas since

Urban development and agricultural practices have led to deforestation, resulting in soil erosion and desertification. Only 3 to 5 percent of the country remains forested, compared with 18 percent in the 1950s.

Greenpeace activists
dredging toxic waste
from the sea.

1966. It also has agreed to conserve and sustain biodiversity as well as protect its wetlands under the Ramsar Convention.

Since 1993, Lebanon has agreed to phase out emissions of greenhouse gas as ratified in the Montreal Protocol and agreed to refrain from adding to the earth's rising temperature as a party to the Convention for Ozone Layer Protection. In 1994 Lebanon ratified the Basel Convention on minimizing the amount of waste generated and the sound management of hazardous waste and also ratified the Convention on Climate Change to set emission limits on greenhouse gas in order to avoid interfering with the natural climate system.

In addition to ratifying the UN Convention on the Law of the Sea, which includes dealing with pollution of the marine environment, Lebanon is also a party to the Marpol Convention on preserving the marine environment by eliminating oil dumping and other harmful pollutants into the sea. Treaties on environmental modification and marine life conservation have been signed but not ratified.

CHOUF CEDAR RESERVE Established in 1997, this is Lebanon's largest nature reserve and occupies 5 percent of the country's total land area. It is home to more than 123,000 acres (49,778 ha) of cedar forests, 200 species of birds, and 26 species of wild mammals, which include wolves and gazelles.

PALM ISLANDS RESERVE A group of islands—Ramkine, Sanani, and Palm Island—in a three-square mile (eight-square km) area make up this sandy haven for the endangered Mediterranean monk seals, rare sea sponges, nesting marine turtles, and migratory birds, among other animals.

Established in 1992, the Palm Islands Reserve is a designated Mediterranean Specially Protected Area under the Barcelona Convention, an Important Bird Area by Birdlife International, and a Wetland of Special International Importance. In the summer months parts of the reserve are open to the public for snorkeling and swimming.

The scenic panorama of the Qadisha Valley in Lebanon is marred by heaps of trash, left there by thoughtless visitors.

TYRE BEACH RESERVE In November 1998 the coastal area of south Tyre, at Ras al-Ain, was established as a nature reserve. The three springs there provide freshwater habitats for sea creatures, and their off-flow creates pockets of marshland enjoyed by amphibians. Many species of birds as well as marine turtles can be found nesting there. Access to Ras al-Ain beach is restricted to provide minimal disturbance to wildlife.

59

LEBANESE

LEBANESE CITIZENS TODAY are mostly descendants of a mixture of peoples—the Phoenicians, Greeks, Crusaders, and Arabs—who at different times occupied the country. It was only after World War I (1914–18), when Lebanon began to define itself as a separate country under French rule, that people even began to think of themselves as Lebanese. In the previous centuries, under Ottoman rule, people in the area thought of themselves as belonging first to the Ottoman state, then to the region in which they lived.

It was also under French rule that the idea of belonging to a religious group was politicized. When the civil war broke out in l975, a resident was defined as a Muslim Lebanese or a Christian Lebanese.

The notion of one nation called Lebanon with one set of citizens almost disappeared. Only since the 1990s have people been allowed to think of themselves, once again, simply as Lebanese.

Above: **Lebanese people taking an evening stroll along the seafront in Beirut.**

Opposite: **Lebanese of Arab descent walking along the Promenade, Beirut.**

ETHNIC MAKEUP

Well over 90 percent of the population, including Muslims and Christians, are Arabs. Because the description "Arab" is sometimes understood to mean "Muslim," not all Lebanese identify themselves primarily as Arabs. Christian Lebanese sometimes prefer to think of themselves as citizens of Lebanon who are Christians, rather than Arabs. The civil war, after all, was largely fought between Christians and Muslims. Some young Lebanese today (both Christians and Muslims) refer to themselves as Phoenicians rather than as Arabs.

Lebanese schoolchildren wearing paper crowns to celebrate Lebanon's Flag Day, which falls on November 21.

Close to 90 percent of Lebanese live in urban areas. The last census in Lebanon was taken in 2003.

In a country that had been torn apart by a civil war for over 15 years, it is not surprising that people have conflicting ideas about how they want to define themselves. Indeed, the whole question of how many Lebanese actually belong to each of the different religious groups is a highly controversial matter.

The largest ethnic minority are the Armenians, who make up 4 percent of the population. They arrived in Lebanon in the early 20th century, escaping massacres in Turkey. In 1924 they were granted citizenship by the French, who wanted to increase the number of Christians in the country. The Armenians have their own language and culture and tend to live together in their own communities in the cities. Like Armenians in other parts of the world, they welcomed the creation of an independent Armenia east of Turkey in 1991.

Assyrians are an ethnic minority group who fled from Iraq in the early decades of the 20th century and, later, from Syria in the 1950s. They are all Christians. There is an equally small number of Kurds, less than one percent of the population. Being Muslims, they have been absorbed into the Arabic culture of the country.

Palestinians are another group of non-Lebanese Arabs living in the country. Many of their ancestors fled from Israel. Most Palestinians now live in camps that often lack basic amenities.

CONFESSIONS

Nearly all Lebanese are Arabs, but they are grouped into what are known within the country as confessions. Confessions are groups based on religion and are the chief means by which Lebanese people identify and define themselves. Indeed, all citizens of Lebanon are required to carry an identity card that states which confession they belong to. It does not necessarily mean that a Christian Lebanese, for example, is a practicing Christian who actually attends church regularly. The confessional categories are more political than religious.

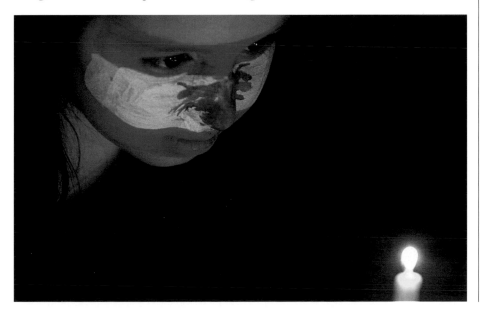

As they struggle to regain their sense of national identity, the Lebanese must learn to cope with the trauma of a civil war that left 125,000 dead and 75,000 with permanent disabilities. Over half a million people left the country during the fighting.

A young Lebanese girl lights a candle in church.

63

ARABS

Lebanon is a predominantly Arab society in terms of both language and culture. A third dimension, that of religion, nearly always contributes to the definition of an Arab society, but Lebanon is an important exception. Nearly all Lebanese speak Arabic as their first language, and there is an Arab culture common to the whole country. But while the Arab world is overwhelmingly Islamic, not all Lebanese are Muslims, and this is very unusual in an Arab society.

Arabs were the original people who lived in the Arabian Peninsula, where Islam was born. As the religion spread, so too did the Arabic language, and the term "Arab" came to represent all those who speak Arabic. Consequently, not all Arabs look alike, and the color of their skin and hair varies widely from light to dark. The Arabs of Lebanon look very much like the Arabs of neighboring Middle Eastern countries and are usually dark-haired with lightly tanned skin.

DRUZES

Druzes are Muslims who live mostly in the mountainous regions of Lebanon and across the border in parts of southern Syria. In language, dress, and many other aspects of daily culture, Druzes are indistinguishable from other Lebanese. It is their religious beliefs alone that make them a distinct group of people within the country. They are influenced by other religions and philosophies in addition to Muslim beliefs, such as Greek philosophy, Gnosticism and Christianity. Like all other Muslims, they do not drink alcohol. Druzes also refrain from smoking: although smoking is not forbidden to Muslims, it is discouraged.

MARONITES

Most Christians in Lebanon are Maronites, an offshoot of the Eastern Orthodox Catholic Church. They have lived in the country since the fifth century, mostly in the north of Lebanon and in the eastern portion of Beirut. Many Maronites have close links with France and French culture, and they speak French fluently.

A Palestinian mother and her child at the Rashidieh Camp in Lebanon. Many Palestinians in Lebanon are not registered, so it is difficult to estimate their numbers.

PALESTINIANS

Palestinians first arrived in Lebanon in 1948 when the state of Israel was created and large numbers of Arabs were forced to flee north. The international community created the United Nations Relief and Works Agency (UNRWA) to look after them, and they were allowed to build camps on the outskirts of Beirut and other large towns. At first they were registered and entitled to education, health, and other benefits. In the early 1950s this provision came to an end, and unregistered refugees who continued to arrive had no legal status whatsoever.

Today, over half the registered Palestinians still live in camps, often with very poor living conditions, and they face disadvantages in nearly all aspects of their life. It is estimated that within the refugee camps there are over 12 different factions, and most Palestinians have no choice but to yield to the authority of whatever faction happens to control their area. They are also barred from working in most professions, further hindering their ability to survive in Lebanon.

During the first half of the civil war, from 1975 to 1982, Palestinians in Lebanon were heavily involved in fighting against the Christian groups.

They paid a terrible price for this in 1976 when Christian militias in Tel-el-Zaater murdered some 2,500 Palestinian men, women, and children. More massacres took place in Shatila and Sabra in 1982 under cover of invading Israeli troops.

Today, over 400,000 Palestinians, or about 10 percent of the population of Lebanon, have no hope of citizenship either in Lebanon or in a new Palestinian state. The refugees living in camps at Shatila and Sabra have been attacked and massacred on more than one occasion. The camps were last flattened in 1985 after a long siege by Shiite militias. Both camps have been shelled and rebuilt a number of times.

The camps were initially scheduled to be pulled down permanently. The government, as part of its ambitious plan to rebuild Beirut, wished to construct a new sports stadium on the land occupied by 50,000 Palestinians. The demolition did not happen, however, as the stadium was rebuilt on land adjacent to the camp.

Passing the time in a refugee center run by a Lebanese nongovernmental organization.

SHAKING OFF THE STEREOTYPE

A familiar image of a Lebanese is that of a young man armed with lethal weapons, dressed in something resembling a military uniform. Throughout the 1970s and 1980s young men joined the militias that acted as military wings of different religious power groups. In the mid-1980s, in addition to the armies of Lebanon, Syria, the Palestinians, the United States, France, and the United Nations, there were almost 20 militia groups. With so many players, it was not surprising that outside observers were often confused by the civil war in Lebanon.

The motives that led even boys in their early teens to drop out of school and join the militias were not always clear-cut. It was not uncommon that these young men did not even know what their militia stood for. What they did see was an economic opportunity (members of militias were paid a regular wage), the offer of protection from rival militias, and a sense of belonging and power. These factors often played a more important role than politics. The grim reality was their easy access to arms and the frequent use of them. Teachers, for example, are sometimes threatened by armed students or militia soldiers.

A Lebanese soldier on deployment to Tyre in south Lebanon puts a flag on a bridge before crossing the Litani River.

When the main opposition to the Taif Agreement was defeated in October 1990 and the civil war ended, the militias slowly disbanded and put down arms, with the exception of the Hizbollah, which provides unofficial military defense in south Lebanon.

LEBANESE DIASPORA

A diaspora is the spread of an ethnic group beyond the borders of its own territory. There is a long tradition, going back several centuries, of Lebanese people migrating to other countries.

The earliest generation of Lebanese migrants was mostly male and largely Christian. Many worked as peddlers. Such a job required very hard work but little capital, and from such humble beginnings many Lebanese established successful lives far from the eastern Mediterranean. As early as the first decade of the 20th century, it was estimated that over 40 percent of Lebanon's foreign earnings came from money sent home by Lebanese abroad. The successful emigrant often returns to Lebanon to retire.

Some 20 years ago there were about one million Lebanese nationals living overseas, and most of them were Christians. During the civil war the number of people leaving the country increased, and both Muslims and Christians left. Between 1975 and 1987 well over half a million people, mostly professionals or semiskilled laborers, left the country. At some point during the civil war in Lebanon, nearly one in four Lebanese were living abroad. In 2004 the Lebanese diaspora abroad numbered about 14 million.

People leave Lebanon primarily for economic reasons. They go to countries where there are employment possibilities. The United States, Brazil, Australia, and the United Kingdom have always been popular destinations, but in recent years the oil-rich states of the Middle East have attracted increasing numbers of Lebanese.

A refugee family leaving Lebanon gather at the airport.

One of the earliest mosques in the United States was built in Ross, North Dakota, by Lebanese immigrants.

LIFESTYLE

LARGE MULTICOLOR BILLBOARDS are a familiar sight along the main roads that lead to and from Beirut's airport. For over a decade these billboards depicted young Lebanese men blowing up Israeli tanks. Some of them glorified Hizbollah's suicide bombers. In late 1995, however, the government decided that such pictures were giving visitors a negative image of Lebanon, and more conventional advertisements have replaced them.

Another sign of the new times can be found in the fact that references to "West Beirut" and "East Beirut" are no longer about two halves of a divided city. A Christian storekeeper, when directing a customer to another shop, which may happen to be Muslim-owned, now talks about "another part of town" rather than just "West Beirut."

STARTING AGAIN

The scene looks peaceful and inviting: green countryside, hills in the distance, birds singing in the trees. It is only the ruins of a modern family house and an untended garden that disrupt the idyllic scene. Part of the house may even be occupied if some rooms are safe to inhabit.

In many cases during the long war, people had to abandon their homes at short notice and returned months or years later to find the shattered remains. "We were the last to leave. It was the middle of the night, and our neighbors came and knocked on the door, shouting urgently that we had to go; we could hear guns very close. We left with nothing. If we'd been able to take things with us, we would have been

Above: **A sculpture named "Hope For Peace" by Lebanese sculptor Armand Fernandez in Beirut.**

Opposite: **Lebanese teens enjoying themselves at the beach on a sunny day.**

71

Many people locked up their homes and fled during the civil war in Lebanon. Some of them returned in the early 1990s after fighting had ended.

all right. But we left with nothing and now we've come back with nothing. We thought we'd be gone a few weeks or months. It has been 10 years now." These words of a man from south Lebanon were spoken as he laid some new bricks on a broken wall of his old home. When the wall was repaired, he planned to begin work on his garden.

All over Lebanon, people are still busy rebuilding their homes. A common sight in the countryside is a truck piled with building materials parked beside a partially rebuilt home. Many Lebanese cannot afford to stay in the countryside while they work on their dwellings. The cost of living in Lebanon is high, and housing, if available at all, is expensive. This is why most Lebanese go to Beirut, as it offers the best chance of employment. On weekends and during occasional holidays, families leave the capital and return to their villages for a working holiday.

MAKING FRIENDS

A survey conducted shortly after peace was established in 1992 showed that 52 percent of the Lebanese had their homes completely destroyed, while 27 percent had homes partially destroyed. As Lebanese families continue to rebuild and repair their homes, they are also faced with

the more difficult challenge of reestablishing broken relationships with their neighbors.

Many villages once had clusters of Christians and Muslims living side by side. The civil war polarized relationships, and neighbors fought neighbors. Friends became enemies overnight. Rebuilding a friendship is not always as easy as rebuilding a house because bitter memories remain.

There is, surprisingly, a positive side to the hardship caused by the years of fighting. In many instances people joined together to help their neighbors when they all faced the challenge of survival in terribly harsh conditions. In doing this they were following the age-old custom of friendly solidarity. The Lebanese have many traditional sayings that reflect the importance of being neighborly, including "Joy is for all, and mourning is for all" and "The neighbor who is near is more important than the brother who is far."

A family passing a bombed-out building in Beirut.

Refugee children washing clothes in a school in Beirut's suburbs.

RICH AND POOR

A major factor affecting the kind of lifestyle available to a Lebanese family is the social inequality between the rich and the poor. In many respects this is no different from most countries in the world.

A survey of the quality of life in one of the refugee camps near Tyre, for example, revealed appalling conditions. Sewage as well as contaminated water are just some of the problems that the refugees have to live with. Daily food rations from United Nations relief funds are the only source of comfort for many of the refugees. Others have to compete with Syrian guest workers for a chance to do menial labor for very low pay. Today in Lebanon over 55 percent of all private income goes to one-fifth of the population. The poorest one-fifth of the country, on the other hand, lives on only 4 percent.

Affluence is often open and ostentatious, particularly in the cities. Apartments of the rich are well stocked with appliances, there are many cars on the roads, and children are given music lessons and go to good schools.

Before the war, everything the rich could afford was found in the city center, particularly in Beirut: movie theaters, first-class shops, and good schools and colleges. Encircling the city were the living quarters of the poor and the factories where they worked.

The majority of citizens work very hard trying to maintain a decent life on meager wages, threatened constantly by inflation. The upheavals of the last 30 years have accelerated the migration of people from the countryside into Beirut, aggravating the already overcrowded and poverty-stricken existence of the poor.

LIFESTYLE STATISTICS

Population:	Over 3.8 million (2006 estimate)
Birth rate:	18.52 births per 1,000 of the population (2006 estimate)
Death rate:	6.21 deaths per 1,000 of the population (2006 estimate)
Life expectancy:	70.41 years for men; 75.48 for women (2006 estimate)
Literacy rate:	87.4 percent over the age of 15 can read and write (2006 estimate)
Unemployment rate:	20 percent (2006 estimate)
Occupations:	62 percent in services
	31 percent in industry
	7.3 percent in agriculture (2005 estimate)

A Lebanese girl playing basketball after school.

YOUTH

Lebanon has a fairly well-educated pool of youth, young men and women between the ages of 18 and 35, but the unemployment rate of this group is high. In fact, it is among the highest in the Middle East and North Africa (MENA) region. In a 2001 study it was noted that for the 18–35 age group, female unemployment stood at 23.2 percent and male unemployment at 11.8 percent. A large percentage of those unemployed are university degree holders. Yet a very small percentage of them are employed in managerial or administrative positions.

This inconsistency can be attributed to a few factors. The education system in Lebanon, as in many Arab countries, has dual features. For example, the system is either secular or religious, the subject of study either general or technically specific, and the language taught and used is either native or foreign. With such variance, even highly educated youth may not be able to find suitable employment if their skills and knowledge do not correspond to the needs of the job market. As a result, many have to find employment outside his or her field of study. The practice of cronyism by potential employers is another reason for the high unemployment rate. Suitable candidates for a job may be bypassed in favor of an employer's less qualified acquaintance. It is thus not surprising that Lebanon is facing a brain drain, as almost 300,000 youth are emigrating to greener pastures every year.

In 2000, Lebanon's parliament rejected a bill to reduce the voting age for youth from 21 to 18 years old. This somewhat limits youth participation in Lebanon's political scene. Further, schools and universities play limited roles in supporting political aspirations. However, it is an encouraging fact that many youths have engaged in organized social activities and workshops over the past few years and are exposed to such aspects of political awareness as human rights, environment, and human welfare. With these experiences it is hoped that they will actively cultivate their inclinations toward good governance.

As everywhere, young people enjoy a pleasant time by themselves.

A young Lebanese woman in traditional costume.

A WOMAN'S LIFE

In some areas of Lebanese life the legal system discriminates against women. For example, a man who kills a wife, sister, or mother may avoid conviction if he can prove that the woman committed adultery. A woman is required by law to obtain her husband's or father's permission for a passport. Only males may confer citizenship on their spouses and children. In some cases this means that a child may be born stateless if the mother is Lebanese and the father is stateless, such as being a Palestinian refugee. The child inherits his father's lack of nationality.

Religious groups have beliefs about a woman's role that may influence their laws concerning marriage and family property rights. Sometimes this means that there is discrimination against women. For example, a Sunni inheritance law gives a son twice the share of a daughter. It is also the case that a Muslim man may divorce easily, but a Muslim woman may do so only with her husband's agreement.

DAILY ROUTINE   In rural areas girls grow up expecting to help in the fields as well as to manage all the household chores: washing, cooking, cleaning, and taking care of the children. Their children are likely to have at least 10 years of school, and will grow up expecting greater independence from home. Women in the cities have the same responsibilities, but in urban areas people accept the idea of women working for a salary. However, women make up only 15 percent of the Lebanese workforce, and very few hold positions of power. In recent years only 6 out of 128 seats in parliament were held by women. But women in Lebanon are becoming more highly educated and more are participating in politics. Thus, other Arabs view Lebanese as being quite progressive in their treatment of the role of women.

COSMETICS   Lebanese women sometimes have colorful red and brown patterns on their hands and feet. The effect is created by applying henna, a dye made from the leaves of the henna shrub. Henna is bought in the form of a powder and then mixed with water. It usually comes in red and black. These are then mixed to provide different shades of red. Sometimes the henna is mixed with yogurt, tea, or coffee, instead of just water; the agent used affects the color. After the dye is applied to the skin, but before it dries, lemon juice is sometimes added to darken the final color from a light orange to a dark red or brown. Fine lines show up more clearly.

A Muslim woman wearing a jeweled ring as her sole adornment.

Women sometimes use a sugary solution as a waxing lotion to remove unwanted hair. About one cup of sugar is mixed with half a cup of water and a small amount of fresh lemon juice. The mixture is boiled to make a concentrated syrup and then left to cool on a cold surface. Before it gets too cold the lotion is applied to the skin as a thin layer, then peeled off in the opposite direction of hair growth.

DRESS   What women wear depends on their religion and where they live. Western dressing is apparently preferred in the cities, and some women are very fashionable. In the country, modest long dresses are more common. Outdoors, Muslim women (especially those in rural areas) may wear a garment that covers them from head to toe.

Lebanese farmers planting potatoes in the Bekáa Valley.

RURAL LIFE

About 7 percent of Lebanese work in the country—a relatively low proportion for the Arab world. In the countryside, the extended family has always been the most basic and important form of social organization. As rural folk migrate to towns and cities, they take with them this emphasis on the family network, thus many small businesses in urban areas are run by such small family groups.

Most farms are very small, slightly more than 2 acres (less than 1 ha). They are owned by single families that cultivate the land, and because each farm is so small, the family income usually needs to be supplemented from another source. In the Bekáa Valley the average farm size is larger, around 7 acres (2.8 ha), but the lack of rainfall restricts the types of crops that can be grown.

The traditional farmhouse includes a *liwan* (LEE-wan), a room that opens onto the outside through a large arched doorway. Such houses are

Lebanese women going to work in the Bekáa Valley.

traditionally built of dried mud and straw bricks because it costs too much to cart building stone in by truck. The flat roof of the house is covered with dried mud. During the hot summer months the roof inevitably cracks and fractures. Most families have homemade ladders handy to reach the roof so they can carry out the necessary repairs.

Traditional rural dress for women consists of a loose dress that reaches the ankles, while men wear loose trousers and large shirts. Such loose clothing suits the dry, hot climate.

HOSPITALITY

Family honor is very important and is expressed in various ways. Hospitality functions as a form of honor and is often extended to include a sense of responsibility for one's guest. A visitor to a Lebanese home is always treated graciously, and food is naturally offered as an expression of hospitality.

Visitors to the country are often surprised at the hospitality shown them. A social encounter with one friendly person can easily lead to visits from place to place to meet all the family members and close friends.

VALUES

Sectarianism and the civil war have affected the values held by many Lebanese. The average citizen of the United States has a strong sense of being an American. For many Lebanese, loyalty to family and religion is felt just as intensely as a feeling of nationality. In a country that had been shattered by years of prolonged civil conflict, family solidarity became the only reliable source of stability. An extended family network will collaborate to finance the education of a young relative, for example, and because there is no social security system, the family becomes an essential means of caring for the ill and the elderly.

Honor is highly valued and is often more important than income. Among males, there is a macho element that is not very different from its counterpart in other cultures. It features a keen regard for male prowess and calls for vengeance to address a perceived insult.

CHRISTIAN SCHOOLS

Jesuits (members of a Roman Catholic religious order) arrived in 1625. Together with the Maronites, they established the first schools in Lebanon. In 1820 American Presbyterian missionaries landed in Beirut, and in 1866 they started what was to become the American University of Beirut. Protestant rivalry with Catholicism led to other schools being established by the Jesuits.

These schools taught in Arabic and revived the study of Arabic literature. The achievements of Arab civilization in the past were studied and, aided by Western notions of democracy, helped to kindle demands for political freedom from Ottoman rule.

EDUCATION

The most noticeable difference in education between Lebanon and Western countries such as the United States is the high percentage of private schools in Lebanon. Only primary education is provided free of charge by the government, and it is compulsory for only five years.

Nearly all the secondary schools are funded by private religious groups. Parents who can afford to send their children to private secondary schools will usually also pay for a private primary education.

The prevalence of religious schools does, unfortunately, make it difficult to break down the religious divisions that have separated the Lebanese for so long.

Despite the lack of government-funded schools, the overall literacy rate remains one of the highest in the Middle East. The net primary school enrollment and attendance between 1996 and 2004 was 97 percent.

The school year runs from October to June. Arabic is the major language of instruction. In many private schools lessons are also taught in French or English. Some schools, like the French University of Saint Joseph in Beirut, caters more to Christians, and Muslim Lebanese are less likely to enroll.

The American University of Beirut, founded in 1866 as the Syrian Protestant College, provides education for all, regardless of religion.

83

RELIGION

ABOUT 60 PERCENT OF ALL LEBANESE are Muslims, and there are five legally recognized Islamic groups. Of these, the Shiite, Sunni, and Druze are the most important sects in Lebanon.

Christians make up 39 percent of the population, and more than half of them are Catholic. There are 12 legal Christian denominations. Major Christian groups include the Maronite Catholic and the Greek Orthodox. The remaining 1 percent of religions includes non-Christian minorities like the Baha'is and Jews.

In all, there are 18 recognized Islamic and Christian sects in Lebanon. The way each group defines itself and its relationships with other religious groups is known in Lebanon as confessionalism. The more common word in other countries to describe this kind of social organization is sectarianism.

Opposite: **Muslim Lebanese schoolgirls wearing head scarves.**

Left: **A Christian Lebanese soldier kneels to pray.**

ISLAM

The Islamic faith originated in Arabia in the early seventh century through the Prophet Muhammad. Followers of Islam are known as Muslims, and their religion is a comprehensive one, covering nearly every aspect of life.

The religion is based on the observance of five pillars: the creed, the performance of prayers, the giving of alms, the observance of fasting, and the performance of the hajj, a pilgrimage to Mecca.

THE CREED The Islamic creed is summed up in these words: "There is no God but God and Muhammad is the Prophet of God." The Islamic faith includes a belief in angels as messengers of God, in prophets who receive messages from God, and in holy books that express those messages. Muslims also believe in a last day of judgment that will be announced by the archangel Asrafil blowing on a trumpet. After judgment all people will go either to paradise or to hell.

The Koran, the holy book of Islam, gives the names of 28 prophets, of whom Muhammad was the last. Twenty-one of the prophets, including Jesus, are also mentioned in the Bible. Unlike in Christianity, where Jesus is given divinity as the son of God, Jesus is just one of the prophets in Islam. The scriptures of Abraham, the Torah of Moses, the Psalms of David, and the Gospels of the New Testament are also believed to be prophetic revelations of God.

PRAYER Islam calls for a Muslim to pray at least five times a day: at dawn, noon, late afternoon, sunset, and night. Worshippers are called to prayer by a mosque official, the muezzin, traditionally from the top of the minaret of a mosque. These days, the calls are usually a recording broadcast through an amplifier.

There are some fascinating overlaps between Islam and Christianity in Lebanon. Worshippers from both religions esteem the Virgin Mary, and texts that predate Christianity by over 2,000 years mention a Virgin Lady. The Lady of Lebanon and the Virgin of Lebanon are mentioned in the texts from Ugarit, an ancient port city north of Syria, that date from around 1400 B.C.

Muslims can pray in a mosque, but this is not obligatory or always practical. Some public buildings have a small room reserved for prayers. Friday is the most holy day of the week, akin to the Christian Sunday, and on that day Muslim men will try to attend a mosque for their prayers. Women usually pray at home, but those who choose to pray at the mosque may do so in a section set aside for them.

Prayers begin by a ritual washing of the body to show one's willingness to be purified. Physical contact with a member of the other sex is not permitted until after prayers, and if a Muslim man accidentally touches a woman, he must wash himself ritually once again before praying. The same goes for a woman if she accidentally touches a man.

Sunni Muslims kneeling down to pray on a Friday at the mosque.

The worshipper always prays in the direction of Mecca and makes a prearranged cycle of prayers. The prayers usually consist of passages from the Koran. Muslims prostrate themselves on a prayer mat in a series of different positions for each of the five daily prayers.

GIVING ALMS Muslims who earn a certain minimum salary must donate 2.5 percent of their wealth to the poor. Muslims also pay a contribution during the fasting month of Ramadan, and even newborns are not exempted from this contribution. The religious authority appoints mosque officials to make this annual collection at the appropriate time. The amount may vary every year, since it is tagged to the cost of staple foods.

FASTING Fasting takes place during the month of Ramadan when no food or drink may be consumed between sunrise and sunset. Among the other prohibitions are smoking during the fasting hours and thinking or speaking ill of others. Only those who are ill, menstruating, or very young are exempted from the fast. Some Muslim children are trained to fast from the age of 7, when they usually fast for half a day. By about the age of 9 or 10, they are ready for full-day fasts. Every night during Ramadan, in the mosque or at home, the Sunni Muslims go through the ritual of a special prayer in addition to the evening prayer.

THE SIXTH PILLAR OF ISLAM

Some Muslims say that the sixth pillar of Islam is jihad, which translates as "striving in the way of God." It is a much misunderstood term that is open to more than one interpretation. Consequently, its intention has been much argued about within the Islamic community.

It is often rendered in English as "holy war." Jihad can mean a holy war against the godless, but it also applies to a holy war by an individual against one's own unholy instincts. In this latter sense it has some similarity with the Christian idea of an individual's striving to be good and struggling with his own conscience.

PILGRIMAGE TO MECCA The pilgrimage to Mecca, or hajj, is an obligation that all Muslims who can afford it do at least once in their lifetime. The traditional month for the big pilgrimage is the last month of the Islamic calendar. (Smaller pilgrimages may be made at any time of the year.) The pilgrimage leads to the forgiving of a Muslim's past sins.

Muslims make careful preparations for their pilgrimage, some as early as a year prior to leaving. Clearing all financial obligations and making sure their family members have been provided for are religious requirements. Special classes conducted by religious teachers coach would-be pilgrims in the rites, prayers, and rules. Pilgrims to Mecca dress in simple white unhemmed clothing called *ihram* (EE-ha-ram), meaning "godly raiment."

Left: **An aerial view of the yearly holy pilgrimage to Mecca undertaken by some Muslims all around the world.**

Opposite: **A Muslim woman diligently reading her Koran.**

SHIITES

Shiism is a religious movement that traces its descent back to the murder of Ali, the son-in-law and cousin of the Prophet Muhammad. Followers who supported Ali's claim to be the next leader after Muhammad died became known as Shi'i (followers of Ali). This is usually anglicized as Shiites.

The most important Shiite group is the "Twelver" Shiites, who believe that there were 12 holy men after Muhammad—Ali and his descendants. They believe that the twelfth holy man did not die and will return one day as savior of the world.

In Lebanon the Shiites tend to be the poorer citizens of the country and mostly share a farming background. In recent years, many Shiites have moved upward economically, becoming part of the middle class.

A crowd of Hizbollah Shiites participating in a religious festival.

DRUZES

The Druzes are an Islamic group that emerged in the 11th century as a branch of the Shiite sect. Shiite Islam has always been more mystical than the mainstream Sunni religion, and this mysticism is found among the Druzes. The Druzes believe in reincarnation. Druze Muslims do not seek or accept converts. They believe in protecting the secrets of their religion and will worship as conventional Muslims when in a non-Druze Muslim community or even as Christians when in a Christian community.

The Druzes believe that God has taken various incarnations as a living person on earth, including that of Jesus Christ, and that he last took human form as al-Hakim in the 11th century. The name of the religion is thought to derive from al-Darazi, a follower of al-Hakim.

Today there are about 2.3 million Druzes worldwide and slightly over 5 percent are in Lebanon. As a general rule they marry only among themselves. They do not worship in a mosque but meet for prayers on Thursday evenings in a house close to their particular village.

A group of Druze men indulge in casual conversation while waiting for prayers to begin.

91

Lebanese Catholics lighting candles before Mass.

SUNNI MUSLIMS

Sunni is the mainstream sect of Islam found throughout the Middle East. Over 80 percent of all Muslims in the world are Sunnis. They do not accept the Shiite belief about Muhammad's successor, although they still respect Ali and firmly believe he was a "rightly guided leader." Because Sunnis form the majority, their view is the orthodox one.

In Lebanon the Sunnis traditionally are settled in the Mediterranean coastal cities of Beirut, Tripoli, and Sidon. Most of the Palestinian refugees in Lebanon are also Sunnis.

CATHOLICS

The most important Christian groups in Lebanon are Uniate Catholics, which means the members accept the authority of the pope in Rome but practice their own particular rites. They include the Maronites, Greek Catholics, and Armenian Catholics.

The Greek Catholics are also called Melchites. They are the descendants of a Greek Orthodox community that broke off from the Greek Orthodox Church in the 18th century. They retain many of their Greek rites but accept the authority of the pope in Rome, which the Greek Orthodox Church members do not. Today many Melchites live in the town of Zahlé.

The Armenian Catholics are distinguished by their usage of Greek in religious ceremonies. They came to Lebanon to escape the massacres of Armenians by the Turks around the time of World War I.

THE MARONITE CHURCH

The Maronites are Catholics who are traditionally associated with the northern part of the country, although they also live in southern Lebanon. They originated in Syria in the early seventh century and shortly after moved into Lebanon.

They take their name from Saint Maron, a fourth-century monk. Originally the Maronites were monothelite, believing that Christ has one will but two natures, but in the 12th century they grew closer to mainstream Roman Catholicism. They elect their own church leader, a patriarch, through their bishops, and if the bishops cannot agree on a choice within 15 days, the pope in Rome makes an appointment.

In 1736 the Maronites became affiliated with the Roman Catholic Church, and this provided Catholic France with an excuse to ally itself with them in Lebanon. The Turkish government retaliated by supporting and encouraging the heretical Muslim group, the Druze, as a counterweight to France's influence. Today the number of Maronites in Lebanon is estimated to be around 640,000 to 850,000. Traditionally, Maronites have identified themselves with the West, as they did in the time of the Crusades.

CHURCHES AND MOSQUES

The history of religion in Lebanon can be traced in its architecture. The Grand Mosque of Umar in Beirut has foundation stones from the Roman and Byzantine eras, when the building was a Christian church. It was a Christian cathedral during the Crusades. In the 13th century it was converted into a mosque. The Great Mosque in Tripoli has a similar history. It dates from the 14th century but incorporates parts of the earlier Christian cathedral of Saint Mary of the Tower. The Italian-style minaret of the mosque is believed to be the original bell tower of the cathedral.

LANGUAGE

NEARLY ALL LEBANESE speak and write Arabic. The most important second languages are French and English. English is more important than French for international business, but the legacy of French rule in Lebanon has ensured that French is still more commonly spoken than English. Armenian is the most established minority language and it is spoken by the relatively small number of Armenians who arrived in Lebanon around the time of World War I, fleeing Turkish massacres.

ARABIC

Arabic, the everyday language for nearly all Lebanese, is spoken by over 300 million people around the world. As the name suggests, it was originally the language of Arabia, and as Islam spread beyond Arabia in the seventh and eighth centuries, so did the language of the religion.

Arabic has more than one form. The spoken form, as used by people in their everyday lives, is known as colloquial Arabic. The various Arabic-speaking countries each have their own forms of colloquial Arabic. A Lebanese speaks Arabic and so does an Egyptian, for example, but their Arabic is not identical and the speakers cannot always easily communicate. The Lebanese speak in Levantine Arabic, a dialect strongly influenced by Syriac and Aramaic Arabic. Within Lebanon itself, Arabic dialects differ from region to region, with the Druze having the most distinct dialect. In the more remote mountainous regions in the eastern part of the country,

Above: **A McDonald's signboard stands out against the bustling cityscape.**

Opposite: **A Beirut Green Line redevelopment sign with English and Arabic lettering.**

SECTEUR 66 ٦٦ منطقة

PALAIS DES JUSTICE العدلية

RUE 17 ١٧ شارع

Arabic is written from the right to the left. Classical Arabic is used in books and newspapers and is understood by literate Arabs everywhere, not only in Lebanon.

there are local dialects that do not have a written form. These are used only for communication within the local group, affecting geographically small areas.

Classical Arabic is quite different. It is the language of the Koran and provides a common and shared written form for all Arabic speakers.

A third form of Arabic, the Modern Standard Arabic (MSA), is a mixture of the first two. In its spoken form it provides a shared language for all Lebanese and also facilitates communication between the Lebanese and other Arabs.

Arabic belongs to the diglossic languages, or languages with significant differences between spoken and written forms, and it is regarded as a difficult language to learn. Lebanese linguists are working on the compilation of a Lebanese dictionary, one that lists words by theme rather than in the traditional ordering system of Arabic that groups words according to their linguistic roots.

ENDANGERED DOCUMENTS

The Sherfe monastery on the hills north of Beirut has the world's sixth-largest library of manuscripts. Its collection of over 3,000 manuscripts, dating from the 11th to the 19th centuries, is considered one of the most important in the world after the collections of the British Museum, the Vatican, and the national libraries in Paris, Berlin, and Saint Petersburg.

The collection in the Sherfe monastery includes the diary that Michael the Syriac kept during the 11th century to chronicle the Crusaders' expeditions in the Middle East. Unfortunately, due to atmospheric conditions and the relentless activity of insects, priceless documents like Michael's diary are disintegrating. Although the diary and other ancient documents are kept in glass cabinets in two dark rooms of the ancient monastery, they are now too fragile to be consulted or even touched.

Some of the manuscripts were written in Syriac, an ancient language related to Aramaic and considered to be the dialect spoken by Christ. Syriac scholars also wrote in Arabic, and between the 8th and 13th centuries they translated into Arabic the works of Aristotle and Plato. The texts in Arabic went to Spain (when the Arabs ruled Spain), where they were translated into Latin, thus providing a cultural foundation for the European Renaissance, between the 14th and 17th centuries.

The Sherfe library was established in 1780 by the visionary founder of the monastery, Monsignor Ignace Michel III Jarwa. Some of his monks were given the assignment of tracking down original manuscripts that were scattered around the eastern lands of the Ottoman Empire. They were sent out with funds to purchase manuscripts and in the event a sale could not be arranged, had the task of copying the entire manuscript so that a copy might be preserved in the monastery library. Without the work of the monks from the Sherfe monastery, many important documents would have been lost forever.

Arabic became established as the chief language of Lebanon under the Abbasid dynasty (750–1258).

THE POLITICS OF LANGUAGE

With the civil war behind them, the Lebanese are more concerned today with getting ahead. Since English is perceived as the language of the business world, Lebanese parents are now pushing their children to take English-language classes.

Language is more than just a means of communication in Lebanon. A person's choice of language has a symbolic importance that is usually related to politics. For example, Muslim Lebanese use Arabic to signify a link to their fellow Arabs, while some Christians use French rather than Arabic to indicate their political opposition to Muslim groups. This may not always be political, however, as some Christian Lebanese simply speak French because they were educated in French schools.

Some Maronite groups would prefer schools to adopt the Lebanese colloquial dialect of Arabic instead of teaching classical Arabic. Those who have little sympathy for Arab nationalism perceive the use of classical Arabic as a tool of Arab nationalists. If Lebanon adopts its colloquial form of Arabic as the national language, it would be seen as distancing itself from the rest of the Arab world. This is very unlikely to happen.

Even names tend to signify one's religion in Lebanon. Popular Muslim names are Muhammad (also spelled Mohammed and Mohammad) and Ahmad, while French names like Pierre and Michel are likely to be chosen by Christians. Biblical names like Sarah may belong to either a Christian or a Muslim.

A ROSE BY ANY OTHER NAME

It often happens that Arabic words have more than one spelling when transliterated into English. For example, the Arabic musical instrument from which the European lute is derived appears in writing as both 'ud and oud, both pronounced in the same way (OOD). Another example is the Muslim sect known both as the Druze and the Druse.

Transliteration from Arabic to English is difficult for two reasons: there are sounds in Arabic with no equivalent in English, and there are vowel sounds in spoken Arabic that do not appear in written Arabic. Because there is no agreed-upon system for transliteration, words regularly appear with different spellings.

BODY LANGUAGE

Gesturing is a natural part of conversations all over the world, whatever the language, but the meanings of similar gestures vary from one culture to another. Common gestures found in Lebanon are fairly typical of the Middle East as a whole. People may express a simple negative, "no," by raising the eyebrows and lifting the head up and back a little. Such a gesture is often accompanied by a "tsk tsk" noise. In some parts of the world this noise usually expresses disapproval or a snub, but not in the Middle East.

Shaking the head from side to side does not mean "no," but "I do not understand." Stretching out a hand as if to open a door, while at the same time flicking the wrist and hand, can mean "What is the problem?" or "What do you want?" It often functions as a general expression of inquiry.

The right hand held over the heart usually means "No thank you." A traditional female greeting in Lebanon is raising the right hand and lightly touching one's chest. It is an Islamic gesture. Many younger Lebanese nowadays simply greet each other with a handshake. In most social intercourse the right hand is used to give or receive anything.

Men hold hands as a gesture of friendship or simple companionship. A male stranger asking for directions may be taken by the hand and shown the right direction.

In conversation, urban Lebanese switch easily from Arabic to English to French, and they use hand gestures freely.

ARTS

LEBANON HAS A TRADITION in the arts that is as ancient as its monuments. Lebanese literature has been translated and widely disseminated, and the works of such Lebanese-born writers as Kahlil Gibran and Amin Maalouf are familiar to readers around the world. Before the civil war the art scene in Lebanon, particularly in traditional music and dance, was the toast of the Middle East, and the international festival in Baalbek had global acclaim.

ANCIENT ART

Lebanon is justly proud of the many architectural and other artistic remains that make up its most celebrated artistic heritage. The National Museum in Beirut has an especially rich collection of ancient art, dating far back to terra-cotta figures of 3000 B.C. There are also Phoenician figures from around 1600 B.C. Adornments on many of these figures—such as the way hair is braided or a rich array of bracelets—reveal the influence of Egypt. Phoenician jewelry also shows the inspiration of Egyptian art, including a fondness for amethyst, a semiprecious violet-to-purple form of quartz.

One of the most highly regarded objects in the National Museum is an 11th century B.C. hand-carved sarcophagus made for the king of Byblos. The king is shown holding a lotus blossom and enthroned between two sphinxes, mythological monsters with human heads and lions' bodies. The sphinx originated in the East, probably in Egypt, and is commonly found in ancient art from the eastern Mediterranean region. What really makes the sarcophagus outstanding is a carved alphabetic inscription that is one of the very earliest appearances of writing in the world.

Above: **Lebanon is fortunate in possessing good examples of art from historic periods, such as this hunting scene carved in stone from Baalbek.**

Opposite: **Lebanese people dressed in traditional costumes in a folkloric festival, Beirut.**

101

BEIT ED-DIN

The palace at Beit ed-Din, some 30 miles (50 km) from Beirut, is the best example of 19th-century Lebanese architecture to be found anywhere in the country. It was built for the Emir Beshir, who governed Lebanon for 50 years, and its construction took 30 years.

The palace is filled with porticoed courts, arcades, and fountains. The ceilings and walls were richly decorated by the best craftsmen in the country, using tiny pieces of mirror to create intricate mosaic designs in glass.

BAALBEK Baalbek (Baalbeck) is a small town in the Bekáa Valley, near the Anti-Lebanon Mountains. It is world famous for its imposing Greco-Roman ruins, including a temple to the ancient Greek god Dionysus (called Bacchus by the Romans). In the seventh century Arabs turned Baalbek into a military base and built over the top of many of the existing ruins. Paradoxically, this helped to preserve archaeological remains by keeping them a secret for a very long time.

The Dionysus temple has magnificent stately columns built from gigantic blocks of locally quarried stone, measuring 62 by 14 by 11 feet (19 by 4 by 3 m). The builders of Baalbek also used pillars of rose granite imported from Egypt. It has been estimated that it took some three years for the granite to be transported and erected at Baalbek.

The temple site of Dionysus, or Bacchus, in Baalbek.

Delicate sculptures in Baalbek depict lines of twining vines and other plants, including poppies and wheat. There is a sculpture of the Greek sun god, Helios, from which the town's earlier name, Heliopolis, or "city of the sun" came about (not to be confused with the Heliopolis of ancient Egypt).

EXCAVATING ART The multibillion-dollar rebuilding of Beirut has unearthed ancient art and artifacts going back to Phoenician times, some 2,500 years ago. The work done by archaeologists is painstaking and slow. They may use toothbrushes to unearth evidence of a Phoenician neighborhood nearby, while bulldozers are used in the laying of sewer pipes and electrical cables for the new Beirut. So far, more than 1.5 million square feet (1 million square m) of land has been excavated

by an international team of archaeologists, making it one of the largest archaeological digs in the world.

The Phoenician neighborhood being excavated includes six houses where fishermen once lived. The narrow streets and arches that they used are still intact in places. Over the top of this Phoenician settlement the Ottomans also built homes. Between 1993 and 1996 a stretch of Ottoman wall 200 feet (60 m) long was among the archaeological finds, along with tombs, kilns for glass and pottery production, and mosaic floors from the Roman-Byzantine period.

The excavation work has also unearthed a treasure trove of antiquities from ancient Roman times: statues, glassware, a whole stretch of road still bearing the marks left by chariot wheels, and, most recently, a bath that has now been partially restored. An inscription on a mosaic has been discovered with the following observation: "Jealousy is the worst of all evils. The only good about it is that it eats up the eyes and heart of the jealous."

Archaeological investigations in Lebanon have unearthed valuable facts about its ancient cities. One of these is that the port of Jbail has been continuously inhabited for about 5,000 years.

An oud maker tests his instrument.

MUSICAL INSTRUMENTS

Traditional instruments include a flutelike instrument called the *nay* (NAY), which is found in many Middle Eastern cultures as well as in North Africa. It is a relatively difficult instrument to play, especially when it is compared with the recorder that it resembles. Only very accomplished musicians can actually play the entire three-octave range of the *nay*. It is more common for musicians to use *nays* of different sizes to span the three octaves.

Traditional musicians also play a drum called the *daff* (DAHF), which resembles a tambourine. Another tambourine-like instrument is the *riq* (reek).

The musical instrument with the most ancient lineage is the oud. It dates back to at least the seventh century and is regarded as the forerunner of the European lute. The oud is the most important musical instrument in Arab culture, and there are a number of slightly different types. It is played with a plectrum (pick) or with the fingers of both hands.

NEW MUSIC FOR NEW TIMES

Lebanon has a tradition of folk music, and children are taught this familiar music from their first year in school. Today, however, new music combining Arabic and Western arrangements, fusion, and pop music, are fast gaining ground.

When car bombings and kidnappings were regular events in Beirut, the lyrics of fusion musician Marcel Khalife reflected this highly charged political atmosphere. He wrote songs that dealt with experiences common for many Lebanese—being interrogated by border guards, for example. His music was regarded with suspicion by many politically powerful officials. To the ordinary people of war-torn Lebanon, however, he was a folk hero who lifted their despair into poetry, often reducing his audiences to tears.

His album *Jadal* is a concerto for two players performed with the *riq* and a bass guitar. Khalife has also composed works for philharmonic

Lebanese musician and singer Marcel Khalife performing live at the Beiteddine Festival in Mount Lebanon.

orchestras, citing 13th-century Arab historians who wrote about ensembles composed for up to 100 musicians. His favorite instrument is the oud.

Arabic pop music first came out of Cairo in the 1970s. It was initially deemed as being one dimensional because of repetitive vocals and the use of only one sound apparatus, the synthesizer. Twenty years later, pop music had evolved, and pianos, guitars, and drums became part of Lebanese pop music. Majida al-Rumi and Diana Haddad are among the more well-known pop music artists. The *4 Cats*, Lebanon's first all female pop group, melds Arab and Western pop. Their first album, *Tic-Tick,* sold more than one million copies and stayed at number one on the Arabic top charts for more than four months.

Lebanese dancers in an array of colorful costumes as they perform a traditional folk dance.

DANCE

The national dance is the *dabke* (DAHB-key), a very energetic five-step folk dance originating in the Bekáa Valley and south Lebanon. Nowadays it is performed throughout the country. It is a historic, living dance, not one preserved for tourists and special cultural shows, and amateur groups are often seen practicing the steps. The Lebanese dance the *dabke* to celebrate their enjoyment of life at any occasion where people gather, from simple family parties to elaborate feasts.

Performances of the *dabke* provide increasingly rare opportunities to see people dressed up in traditional Lebanese mountain dress. When the dance is performed by women, they wear kerchiefs on their heads and brightly colored skirts. The traditional music that accompanies the dance has a distinctive jaunty sound with haunting undercurrents.

The *dabke* has a number of themes that allow for variations in the dance form. They are usually related to aspects of village life such as marriage and disputes over land. The dance was characteristically performed by villagers when the day's work was done.

Lebanon has its own unique dance troupe, called Caracalla. The troupe's performance combines elements of Oriental dance, opera, theater, drama, and even modern literature. They are wildly popular and can be seen performing at some of Lebanon's summer festivals.

Belly dancing, involving sinuous and sometimes vigorous movements of the hips and abdomen, is often seen performed by young women, both informally and at nightclubs.

What most people know as belly dancing actually requires skillful hip movement.

Cow sculptures in an art exhibit in Beirut.

FOLK ART

Many of the folk arts practiced in Lebanon are a mixture of those characteristic of the Levant and the larger Arab world.

In carpet weaving, a well-established craft, the necessary skills and knowledge of time-honored motifs are passed down from one generation to another within a family. The themes and patterns for carpets reveal the influence of the Islamic world, being mainly nonfigurative and favoring abstract but colorful designs.

Filigree ornamental work in fine gold wire is a specialty, an offshoot of the jewelry craft that Lebanon is famous for. The motifs found in jewelry designs betray a strong Turkish influence from the Ottoman period. Flowers, birds, and crescents made of semiprecious stones and diamonds are favorite designs.

Artisans who work with precious metals used to do their tool work outside their shops in the bazaar, or souk. Lumps of gold were "pulled" by two or three men who attached the gold to another man's belt and then stretched the gold out as the man with the belt slowly turned in circles, producing the thin gold wire used in many ornaments.

In Lebanon, men customarily specialize in working with gold and metal inlay, and other jewelry. Women, usually those living in the countryside, tend to concentrate on embroidery work in linen, cotton, and lace, and on carpet weaving.

CINEMA

Eloquent testimony to the resilience of Lebanese culture is found in the intelligent, sensitive films that continued to be made throughout the civil war. A good example is *Beirut, the Encounter,* directed by Borhan Alawiya, a 1986 film based on the problems of two victims of religious and political divisions in their country. The man, a Shiite Muslim from the south, and his girlfriend, a Christian who lives in the east, communicate by telephone, but their plans to meet are frustrated by the war. They resort to exchanging cassette tapes to sustain their friendship, but when a real opportunity presents itself for a face-to-face encounter, they avoid it because of their mutual realization that the war has changed their relationship.

Due to a lack of state funding, the postwar film industry is still sluggish. In spite of that, in 1991 a Cannes Film Festival prize was awarded to Lebanese movie director Maroun Bagdadi for *Hors la Vie* (*Out of Life*).

In 1998 *West Beirut*, directed by Ziad Duweyri, won international and local acclaim for the story about a teenager living in West Beirut during the first year of the civil war. In the same year a documentary about life in the refugee camp Shatila, *Children of Shatila*, by Mai Masri, was nominated for the Amnesty International Award.

To ease the film industry back into the international scene, Docudays, a documentary festival, and the Beirut Film Festival are held annually to encourage aspiring film and documentary talents.

LITERATURE

Newspaper and book publishing in Lebanon began sometime in the late 19th century and is linked to the establishment of universities by Christian missionaries in that period.

Among the prominent international novelists in the Middle East is the Lebanese writer Hanan al-Shaykh. Her works have been translated into English, including *Beirut Blues,* her 1995 novel. Another writer is Huda Barakat, whose first novel, *The Stone of Laughter,* has also been translated into English.

Neither al-Shaykh nor Barakat can escape the impact of the civil war that tore apart their country for so long. But neither examines only the conflicting loyalties that drove their countrymen to kill each other. Politics, in the narrow sense of religious and nationalist causes, is of less interest to the novelists than the human landscape revealed by the war. Barakat's novel especially examines matters of gender. *The Stone of Laughter* has a male central character who, as the war proceeds, is sucked into a macho world that eventually leads him to reject his own feminine elements. Some other Lebanese works include Emily Nasrallah's *Flight Against Time, Sitt Marie Rose* by Etel Adnan, and *Unreal City* by Tony Hanania.

Nour Salman is a Lebanese poet who reflects on the bitter legacy of 15 years of civil conflict that witnessed the breakdown of community life. During periods of intense fighting in the cities, the people of Beirut were always aware of the dangers of falling victim to the fighting. They felt like hostages in their own city so that, as Salman expressed it, "We are the inhabitants of the cages." Similar themes are also voiced by such other poets as Khalil Hain and Nadeen Nainy.

Other important Lebanese writers include poets Khalil Gibran, Charles Corm, and Hector Klat; novelists Amin Maalouf and Layla Ba'labakki; political writers Charles Malek and Antoine Najim; and playwright Elias Khoury.

ZAJAL A literary folk tradition, *zajal* (ZAH-jal), is a form of poetry involving a group of poets who take part in a witty dialogue by improvising lines of verse. It is usually sung rather than recited and often forms part of a village festival, often performed while people eat and drink.

BEIRUT BLUES

Hanan al-Shaykh's novel *Beirut Blues* takes the form of a series of 10 letters written to friends and public figures by the central female character, Asmahan. The background to all the letters is the civil war, which is described as raging in the "demons' playground" of Lebanon but drawing to an end as it "dies of weariness."

One of the letters in the novel is written to Asmahan's idol, American blues and jazz singer Billie Holiday. The blues is a music of lament, sad but resilient, and a comparison is made between Holiday and a Lebanese singer, Ruhiyya. The American singer "heard the blues played again and again on records rising and falling and spinning like globes in circular seas," while Ruhiyya "heard them from minarets and in the songs of the Shia [Shiite] martyr's passion plays." The singers are seen to have something important in common, and West meets East in a cultural duet: "Neither of you resorted to the pen. . . . Instead you both sing the reality you live."

PRIZEWINNER

Amin Maalouf is a Lebanese writer who left his country in 1976 to live and work in France. Seventeen years later, in 1993, he won the Prix Goncourt, France's most prestigious literary award. He was awarded the prize for his novel *The Rock of Tanios*, a love story set in early 19th century Lebanon.

The winner of the Prix Goncourt receives the princely sum of 50 francs—less than $10—but the award bestows the assurance of international renown and attention and, hopefully, increased sales of one's prize book.

LEISURE

SOCIAL LIFE AND LEISURE TIME in Lebanon are based primarily around the family. This does not mean, however, that Lebanese people wish to keep to themselves and their close family members only. Socializing with others is very important and enjoyable to most Lebanese and is usually accompanied by a degree of hospitality seldom found in the West.

THE FAMILY

Many Lebanese homes are organized around the extended family, with grandparents often living with one of their children and his or her family. Other married children and their families join this extended family on festive and holiday occasions, considerably enlarging the family group.

Partly due to the disruption caused by the years of fighting, and partly because Lebanese people have a long tradition of traveling abroad for work and study, it is difficult for families to get together. In recent years there has been a continuous migration of people from the countryside to Beirut and to large cities; this has also caused many families to be separated. When there is a holiday or free time, families want to be together, and reunions become an important leisure goal for many Lebanese people, young and old.

Opposite: **Young and old Lebanese having a day of fun at the beach.**

Below. **A Lebanese family on an outing in Sidon.**

A Lebanese man reclining comfortably while enjoying his afternoon water pipe.

SOCIALIZING

Spending part of the day with an acquaintance or two and whiling away the time in casual conversation is a popular leisure activity. The scene

THE IMPORTANCE OF CIVILITY

Civility has been refined to an art in Lebanon. When people congregate to socialize, even in an informal situation, they often begin the encounter with a number of greetings. This may not seem very different from social encounters in the West, but in practice it is more prolonged and formal. Various greetings are made, followed by a reciprocal response to each, with slight variations in the words according to the genders of the participants. Mutual inquiries about health are also exchanged. This behavior reflects the importance attached to civility in Middle Eastern culture.

A common exchange begins with "*As salaamu alaykum*" (as-sah-LAHM-u ah-LAY-koom), which means "Peace be with you." The usual response is "*Wa alaykum as-salaam*" (wah a-LAY-koom ah-sah-LAHM), or "And upon you be peace."

Lebanese partygoers enthusiastically move to the rhythms of the latest dance hit in one of Beirut's popular clubs.

pictured above is sometimes used in tourist literature to represent a typical aspect of the country's culture: men sitting in a café sipping tea or coffee, or perhaps sucking on a *nargileh* (water pipe), and chatting while playing a game of cards or backgammon. Every town has at least one café where men of all ages meet to socialize. However, women do not usually visit cafés; their socializing is more likely to take place in the home.

A NIGHT OUT

Young Lebanese people enjoy American and French music, as well as movies from those countries. The movies are usually shown in their original language with subtitles in Arabic.

In the past Beirut was famous for its active and cosmopolitan nightlife. Now that the war is over and normality is beginning to return, many dance clubs and bars have reopened in the capital.

A soccer ball, an empty alley, and a group of spectators—all that is needed for a game!

SPORTS

Soccer is the most popular sport in Lebanon, where it is usually called football. The game is played in urban areas as well as in the countryside. The two major Lebanese soccer teams are the Beirut Nejmeh and the Beirut Ansar. In 2000 Lebanon hosted the Asian Cup finals. Basketball too is increasingly popular in Beirut and other large towns. Playgrounds and school yards often have basketball courts. Ping-Pong is also well liked.

Swimming and such water sports as boating and waterskiing are popular in the warmer months. Paragliding, hiking, and mountain biking are popular in the mountain areas from May to October. Health-conscious people in Beirut who have little time to holiday in resorts, or no money for private clubs, can be seen jogging down the Corniche, a long beachfront walkway popular with anglers and strolling families.

SKIING The six ski resorts in the mountains of Lebanon come alive with skiers between November and May each year when heavy snows cover the mountains. Lebanon's best-known ski resort is at the Cedars in the north, where there is a grove of the famous trees.

Skiing was introduced to Lebanon by a Lebanese engineer who had studied in Switzerland. Upon returning home in 1913, he was so enthusiastic about the sport he had enjoyed in Switzerland that he introduced it to his fellow countrymen. But skiing took off only when the French army later opened a skiing school to train soldiers to patrol mountainous areas not otherwise easily accessible in the winter.

Between 1948 and 1994 Lebanon sent skiers to every Winter Olympics. In 1994, however, new Olympic regulations disqualified smaller countries like Lebanon from participating. This has not diminished the appeal of the sport in the country. On a fine Sunday it is not uncommon for 10,000 skiers to take to the slopes.

Two elderly Lebanese men playing a leisurely game of backgammon.

PASTIMES

These days many Lebanese spend much of their leisure time watching television. Family members also enjoy board games. Lebanese men, in particular, are especially fond of backgammon, which they call *tawleh*, after the table designed especially for the game.

Chess and card games are also popular choices among the Lebanese. Men are often observed sitting outdoors, playing one of these games.

FESTIVALS

THE MOST IMPORTANT FESTIVALS in Lebanon are religious. Between both the Muslim and the Christian communities, there are festivals in most months of the year.

CALENDARS AND FESTIVALS

The calendar used in most of the world is the Gregorian calendar. It divides the year into fixed days and months with an extra day being added every four years (leap year) to allow for the difference between the calendar year of 365 days and the actual time it takes for the earth to circle the sun (which is just a little longer). With the important exception of Easter, most Christian festivals throughout the world are based on the Gregorian solar calendar. Christmas is always on December 25 and New Year's Day on January 1.

Most Muslim festivals follow what is known as a lunar calendar, which is based on the moon's rotation around the earth. There are still 12 months of either 29 or 30 days, but the lunar year is 10 or 11 days shorter than the Gregorian solar year. As a result, Muslim festivals are not held at the same time each year; the dates vary, moving through the calendar and completing a cycle in about 33 years.

RAMADAN

Muslims look forward to Ramadan, the ninth month of the Islamic calendar, which is a month of fasting. They do not see it as something onerous simply to be endured. Fasting during the day provides a reason for feasting at night, and in Lebanon, Ramadan is characterized by joyful and lively nights. The spirit of sharing is evident, and people frequently stay up all night and then sleep until the afternoon.

Opposite: **A woman dancer waving a flag during festivities in Beirut.**

The 12 months in the Islamic calendar are as follows: Muharram, Safar, Rabi 1, Rabi 2, Jumada 1, Jumada 2, Rajab, Shaban, Ramadan, Shawwal, Dhu al-Qadah, and Dhu al-Hijjah.

EID AL-FITR

Eid al-Fitr marks the end of the fasting month. It begins on the first day of the 10th month and lasts four days. It is celebrated by large family meals, which all members of an extended family make every effort to attend. Toward the end of Ramadan, the family home is thoroughly cleaned in preparation for the feast. If there is money for new clothes or new furniture, this is the time when the shopping will be done.

EID AL-ADHA

Eid al-Adha is called the Feast of the Sacrifice because it commemorates Abraham's willingness to sacrifice his son. Eid al-Adha is celebrated to mark the end of the hajj, which is a pilgrimage to Mecca. Muslims slaughter a sheep on the feast day and give a portion of the meat to the poor. Celebrations tend to be quieter than at Eid al-Fitr.

ASHURA

The Shiites mourn the murder of Hussein, the Prophet Muhammad's grandson, in the first 10 days of Muharram. On the last day, many reenact the murder and walk in a procession, viewed by crowds, performing self-flagellation, sometimes with sharp objects that draw blood, in order to recall the pain of Muslims when Hussein died.

Eid al-Fitr is the most festive period of the year for Lebanese Muslims, as it signifies the glorious culmination of a period of spiritual cleansing and purification. The festival period is a very social occasion, and visits are made to the homes of in-laws and close friends.

Left: **Crowds watch Shiite Muslims in a procession, many of them in clothes stained with their own blood.**

Opposite: **A Lebanese woman shops for veils at a market in Beirut, in preparation for Eid al-Fitr.**

Holy week festivities begin before Easter week in Beirut.

CHRISTIAN FESTIVALS

The major Christian festivals of Christmas and Easter are celebrated in Lebanon in the same manner as in the West.

At Christmastime, trees are decorated and presents purchased for family and friends. On December 24, midnight Mass is celebrated in most churches. Churches are packed with worshippers on December 25. It is a prime time for family reunions.

January 6 marks the Epiphany, a religious festival that commemorates the showing of the Infant Jesus to the Magi, the manifestation of the divinity of Christ at his baptism, and his first miracle at Cana. It is still a custom in some places to prepare special Epiphany cakes to mark the occasion. They are also known as finger biscuits because of their shape. A special syrup is made, consisting of sugar, lemon juice, rosewater, and orange-blossom water mixed together and simmered until quite concentrated. The biscuits are soaked in this syrup and then fried in vegetable oil.

Easter is marked by processions. On Palm Sunday, the Sunday before Easter, families parade with their children, carrying branches of palm leaves, flowers, and candles. Easter Sunday begins at midnight with a procession of families, led by a priest, to the front door of their unlighted church. He knocks loudly, calling out for the door to be opened so that the King of Glory can enter. He is refused. He knocks and makes his demand three times before the door is opened and the lights come on.

INDEPENDENCE DAY

Independence Day, November 22, is marked by national celebrations. In a country that has been at war with itself for so long, a day of national celebration is especially appropriate. The day celebrating Lebanon's independence from France had little meaning during the 1980s, but now it has great significance.

Beirut is the center of Independence Day celebrations. The day is a national holiday, and there are parades through the city center. People use the public holiday to visit their families and friends, and celebratory meals are enjoyed.

THE BAALBEK FESTIVAL

Before the civil war erupted in 1975, Baalbek was the location of a major arts festival held between mid-June and early September each year. It was the most prestigious festival in the country and always attracted visitors from all over the world. The success of the festival was partly due to its unique setting, an evocative background of ancient classical ruins, and because of the world-class performances of local and international artists. Performances stopped in 1975 with the outbreak of the war, but in 1997 the Baalbek Festival was revived and resumed its place in the Lebanese calendar of the arts.

Lebanese folk dances—especially the *dabke*, with its themes based on stories of village life—are always featured at the festival. International symphony orchestras and ballet troupes are other regular highlights. An evening ballet performance, with the dancers silhouetted against the temple ruins, is a popular event.

Music festivals are a regular part of Lebanese culture, and historical sites are popular venues. One of the most prestigious music festivals is the one held at Baalbek. Other festivals include the Beit ed-Din music festival; a classical music festival called the Bustan Festival; the Byblos Festival, featuring musical performers from around the Mediterranean; and the Tyre Festival.

FOOD

LEBANESE FOOD SHARES MANY CHARACTERISTICS with the cuisines of other Middle Eastern countries. Common ingredients include lamb, eggplant, chickpeas, yogurt, garlic, mint, and olive oil combinations. In Lebanon, however, they are combined and prepared in ways that help to make Lebanese food especially delicious.

FAVORITES

Three dishes form the staples of many meals: falafel, hummus, and *fuul*.

Falafel is a dish of deep-fried balls of chickpea paste mixed with spices and pickled vegetables or tomatoes. It is usually eaten as a sandwich made with unleavened bread. The meat equivalent of the sandwich is *shawarma* (shah-WAHR-mah). Food stalls serving these are often found on city sidewalks. The meat for *shawarma* is sliced off a vertical spit and then squeezed into the bread and covered to overflowing with pickled vegetables or tomatoes.

Hummus, like falafel, uses chickpeas ground into a paste, but this dish is mixed with lemon, sesame oil, and garlic. It is not as spicy as falafel. *Fuul* (FU-ul), a paste made from fava beans, garlic, and lemon, is often eaten with the oil used to cook it.

Another very popular dish, which could lay claim to being the national dish, is kibbe, sometimes also spelled kibbeh or kibbih. It is usually made from balls of ground lamb and cracked wheat, which are often stuffed with more meat before being deep-fried with onions.

Above: **Lebanese cuisine consists of a wide variety of delicious, tasty dips, vegetables and bread.**

Opposite: **A fruit and vegetable street market in Beirut.**

MEALS

Lebanese lunches and dinners tend to be leisurely affairs. A formal meal begins with an appetizer, often a salad, accompanied by tabbouleh, a delicious mixture of chopped onions, parsley, cracked wheat, and tomatoes. A variety of dips will appear on the table, including hummus, *lebni* (LEB-nee) (a thick yogurt dip), and baba ghanoush, which is made of eggplant.

The main dish is usually lamb, which may be cooked in a variety of ways—stewed with okra, grilled as spicy chops, cubed and grilled on skewers—and nearly always served with rice. Lamb may also be served as *kefta*, spicy ground meat mixed with chopped parsley and onions. After lamb, chicken is the most popular meat.

The traditional accompaniment to most Lebanese meals is an unleavened bread called *khobez* (KOH-bez), usually oval-shaped and always served hot, which is found in many Arab countries. Outside the Middle East this bread is called pita bread. It is used both as a spoon for scooping up food and as a sponge for soaking up sauce or gravy on the plate. An informal meal at lunchtime often consists of cooked ground lamb or chicken sandwiched inside a piece of *khobez* and flavored with onions and spices.

As a general rule, Lebanese meals are not highly structured. There is often no clear distinction between appetizers and main courses. There is certainly no traditional food code that sets out in what order particular dishes can be eaten. People like to mix and match their dishes in an informal manner.

Lebanese family meals tend to be an informal and relaxed affair, such as this family's Sunday brunch.

126

MEZE *Meze* is a varied spread of hot and cold hors d'oeuvres that can include a large number of dishes. There are so many, that when they are all laid out on individual plates, they form a complete and very substantial meal. Some of the more popular dishes include mashed beans; spicy meatballs; dolmas, which are small parcels of rice and meat wrapped in grape leaves; hot and cold salads; seafood; hummus; and pistachios. Another common dish found in a *meze* is grilled shish kebab, or skewered cubes of spiced lamb, peppers, and onions.

A particularly savory *meze* dish consists of crushed almonds, cashews, and walnuts mixed with garlic, onions, cayenne pepper, and spices. It is called *joh mahrouse* (JOH MAH-roose).

ARRACK

Many kinds of wines and spirits are available in Lebanon. If one should look for a "national drink" in the vein of the Greek ouzo or the Turkish raki, then arrack is the Lebanese equivalent. Arrack came into existence around the beginning of the 20th century when absinthe (a bitter anise-flavored liqueur popular in the 1800s) became illegal. Arrack is a potent rumlike brew flavored with aniseed and served mixed with water and ice. Tradition dictates that the water is added before the ice to prevent the formation of "skin" on the surface of the drink.

Arrack, an acquired taste, is a great accompaniment to many Lebanese cuisines. Arrack averages about $6 a bottle for the cheaper varieties. Better varieties that take longer to mature, from six to ten months, are naturally more expensive. Although arrack is not known for giving drinkers hangovers, it is potent and can get one drunk rather easily. Massaya, Ksara, and Le Brun are some of the good local brands.

Above: **Cardamom is a highly aromatic herb that is used to add a little spice to a potent cup of Arabic coffee.**

DRINKS

Tea and coffee are the most popular drinks, but both are prepared a lot stronger than their equivalents in the West. Another difference is that both drinks are served in tiny cups. Tea is often served in small glasses, sometimes flavored with mint. A generous amount of sugar is nearly always mixed with the tea. Coffee is also sweetened before serving. Strong Turkish coffee is preferred, and this has a remarkably thick and almost muddy appearance. The last mouthful in a cup is often not drunk, especially by non-Lebanese. This is not surprising, since the dregs have been compared to silt by those unaccustomed to its thickness!

Lebanese enjoy drinking an Arabic coffee too, often flavored with cardamom. It also is served in tiny cups without handles that hold little more than a mouthful. Refills, poured from a silver or brass pot, continue until the drinker signals "enough" by placing a hand over the top of the cup.

The most common alcoholic drink is arrack; when diluted with water, it turns a milky white color. Wine is also made in Lebanon and is drunk with meals by non-Muslims. In rural areas water is the most common thirst quencher.

Dotted around the countryside, at gas stations and in village centers, are earthenware jugs known as *bre* (BREE). These are filled with fresh water and made available to anyone who needs to quench his thirst. Other types of nonalcoholic drinks include fresh fruit and vegetable juices. *Limonada* (LIM-on-AH-DAH) is a fresh lemon drink that is popular, as is *jellab* (jell-AHB), which is made from raisins and served with pine nuts. Various yogurts are other favorite beverages.

EATING OUT

A common sight one sees outside restaurants is a spit for roasting chicken before the final cooking in large ovens. Barbecued chicken is a favorite of the Lebanese. Lamb is often grilled over charcoal, as with kebabs, which are eaten all over the Middle East. The spicy ground lamb is pressed onto skewers before being grilled and then served with bread and a side dish, which is often a salad.

In the city, on the sidewalks or by the roadside, makeshift tables on wheels are found. Each offers some "fast" food that Lebanese stop to buy and savor on the spot to subdue hunger pangs between meals. Breads, falafel, or simply chickpeas flavored with lemon and spices, together with some squares of paper to serve as plates for these ingredients, are all the entrepreneur needs to set up a business.

A Lebanese bread street vendor in Beirut precariously balances his wares as he prepares to set up stall.

KITCHENS

The rural Lebanese householder cooks on a woodstove. For bread, she prepares the dough and then either bakes it at home on top of a hot convex metal dome placed over a wood-fed fire or takes it to the village bakery, where it is baked for a fee. Urban kitchens are like Western ones, with the usual appliances for preparing and cooking food.

FALAFEL

1 pound chickpeas
 (soaked for 24 hours)
1 medium onion, quartered
1 medium potato, peeled and quartered
4 garlic cloves
1 teaspoon ground coriander
1 teaspoon cumin

2 teaspoons salt
½ teaspoon black pepper
½ teaspoon cayenne
1 tablespoon flour
Vegetable oil, for frying
2 teaspoons baking soda

Drain the chickpeas and put them into a food processor or blender. Add the onion, potato, and garlic and process these until the mixture is finely ground. Then add the ground coriander, cumin, salt, pepper, cayenne, and flour and process until they are well mixed. Cover and leave the mixture to rest for two hours. In a large skillet, heat the oil for deep frying. While waiting, add the baking soda to the mixture that has been resting. With dampened hands, form the mixture into 12 Ping-Pong-size balls, and slightly flatten them. Carefully add the patties to the hot oil in the skillet and fry until golden brown; then drain them on paper towels. The falafels can be eaten between bread as a sandwich or with pitas. This recipe makes 12 falafel balls.

MUHALLABIA (LEBANESE ALMOND CREAM PUDDING)

¼ cup rice flour
3 cups milk
1 pinch salt
¼ cup sugar
¾ cup ground almonds
1 tablespoon rosewater
Pistachios or almonds to garnish

In a small bowl, mix the rice flour in ¼ cup of the milk until it makes a smooth paste. Heat the remaining 2¾ cups milk in a pan. After the milk comes to a boil, add in the flour paste, salt and sugar. Cook over medium heat, stirring constantly, until the mixture thickens. It should take about 10 to 15 minutes. Then add the ground almonds and rosewater and simmer for 5 minutes more. Remove the pan from heat and let the mixture cool. Pour into one serving bowl and garnish with either pistachios or almonds.

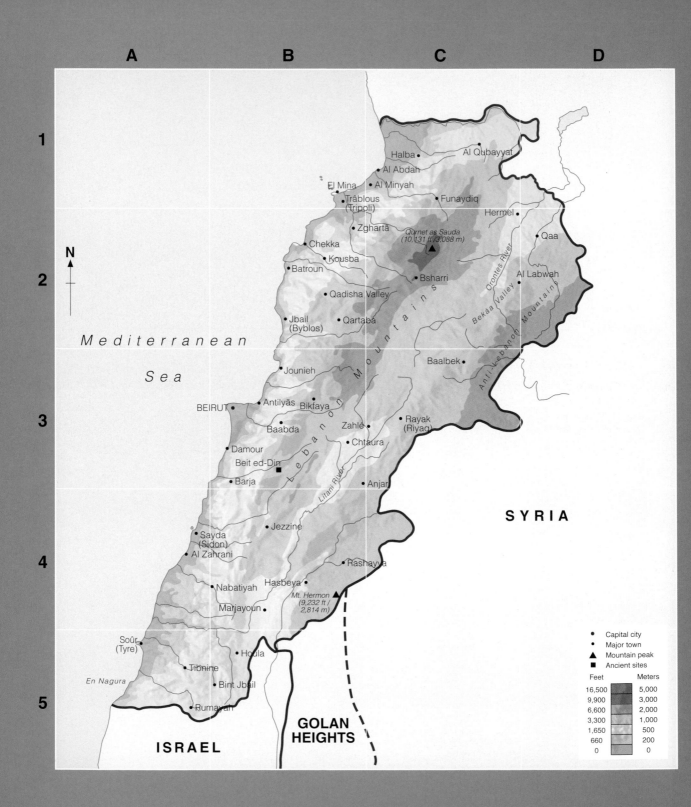

A B C D

1

Halba • • Al Qubayyat

Al Abdah •

El Mina • • Al Minyah

Trâblous •
(Tripoli)

Funaydiq •

Hermel •

Zgharta • Qurnet as Sauda
(10,131 ft /3,088 m) Qaa •

Chekka • ▲

Kousba • Al Labwah •

2

Batroun • Bsharri •

Qadisha Valley

Jbail • Qartaba •
(Byblos)

Baalbek •

Jounieh •

BEIRUT • Antilyâs •
Bikfaya •

3

Baabda • Zahlé • Rayak •
(Riyaq)

Chtaura •

Damour •

Beit ed-Din ■

Anjar •

Barja •

S Y R I A

Jezzine •

Sayda •
(Sidon)

Al Zahrani •

4

Rashayya •

Nabatiyah •
Hasbeya •

Marjayoun • Mt. Hermon ▲
(9,232 ft /
2,814 m)

Soûr •
(Tyre)

Houla •

Tibnine •

Bint Jbail •

5

Rumayah •

Mediterranean

Sea

Lebanon Mountains

Litani River

Bekáa Valley

Orontes River

Anti-Lebanon Mountains

En Nagura

ISRAEL

**GOLAN
HEIGHTS**

N

• Capital city
• Major town
▲ Mountain peak
■ Ancient sites

Feet   Meters
16,500   5,000
9,900   3,000
6,600   2,000
3,300   1,000
1,650   500
660   200
0   0

MAP OF LEBANON

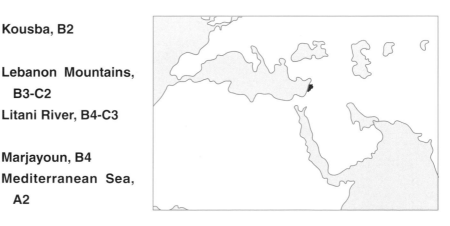

ECONOMIC LEBANON

Manufacturing

 Cement

 Jewelry

 Oil Refining

 Textiles

 Wood & Furniture Products

Agriculture

 Fruits & Vegetables

 Grapes

 Hemp (Hashish)

 Olives

Sheep

Tobacco

Natural Resources

L Limestone

 Iron Ore

Salt

Services

 Airport

 Port

 Tourism

ABOUT
THE ECONOMY

OVERVIEW
After the end of the civil war, extensive borrowing from both local and foreign aid enterprises raised substantial debts that stand at nearly 170 percent of Lebanon's GDP. The Lebanese pound eventually stabilized which led to Beirut's banks attracting billions of dollars worth of foreign investments. Industrial production increased, and agricultural output and exports showed substantial gains. The assassination of former prime minister Rafiq al-Hariri in 2005 slowed down economic activity, but the government soldiered on with economic reforms that include privatization, increasing foreign investment, and restructuring its mounting debts. The economy remains overwhelmingly service-based, accounting for 61 percent of its GDP. Its agricultural sector makes up 12 percent, with industry making up the other 27 percent.

GROSS DOMESTIC PRODUCT
$23.69 billion (2005)

CURRENCY
1 Lebanon pound (LBP) = 100 piastres
Notes: 100,000; 50,000; 20,000; 10,000; 5,000; 1,000; 500, 250; 100 LBP
Coins: 500; 250; 100; 50 piastres
1 USD = 1,513.70 LBP (July 2006)

LAND USE
Arable land 16.35 percent; permanent crops 13.75 percent; others 69.9 percent (2005 estimates)

NATURAL RESOURCES
Limestone, iron ore, salt, water, arable land

AGRICULTURAL PRODUCTS
Citrus, grapes, tomatoes, figs, vegetables, potatoes, olives, tobacco, sheep, goats

MAJOR EXPORTS
Authentic jewelry, inorganic chemicals, various consumer goods, fruit, tobacco, construction minerals, electric power machinery, textile fibers, paper, hemp

MAJOR IMPORTS
Petroleum products, cars, medicinal products, clothing, meat and live animals, consumer goods, paper, textile fabrics, tobacco

MAJOR TRADING PARTNERS
Syria, United Arab Emirates, Turkey, Switzerland, Saudi Arabia, Italy, France, Germany, China, United States, United Kingdom

INFLATION RATE
2.4 percent (2005 estimate)

WORKFORCE
2.6 million (with as many as 1 million foreign workers), (2001 estimate)

UNEMPLOYMENT RATE
14 percent (2000 estimate)

CULTURAL LEBANON

Tripoli—Known as the capital of the north, Tripoli is famous for its lively souks, or traditional marketplaces, and its Crusaders' castle. Historical sites are numerous here.

Qadisha Valley—Included in the UNESCO World Heritage List, Qadisha Valley is lush, serene, and dotted with ancient monasteries, cave shelters, and churches.

Byblos—One of the world's most ancient, continuously occupied cities with impressive archaeological remains. Byblos is also known for its beautiful stone buildings with red tile roofs.

Beirut—Lebanon's capital has a dynamic commercial and social life. Visitors will see the ambitious postwar reconstruction in Beirut Central District and the Beirut National Museum, where Lebanon's archaeological treasures are housed.

Tyre—A major seaport center in ancient Phoenicia, Tyre is also the site of one of antiquity's largest Roman stadiums.

Baalbek—Famous for its lavish and well-preserved temples of ancient Rome. One of these is the Temple of Jupiter, with its six still standing Corinthian columns towering 72 feet (22 m) high.

Zahlé—Wadi el-Aarayesh (Grape Wine Valley) is the site of Lebanon's famous open-air restaurants. It is also the wine center of Lebanon. Every year, between the 10th and 20th of September, the Festival of the Vine is celebrated.

Anjar—Founded in the eighth century by Caliph Walid I, the city of Aanjar was exclusively an Umayyad stronghold. Their rule left behind majestic ruins evident of skilled city planning.

Sidon—The largest city in south Lebanon, with picturesque fishing ports and numerous old souks. The city is also dotted with many caravansaries, or inns, built by Fakhreddine II in the 17th century for traveling merchants and goods.

ABOUT
THE CULTURE

OFFICIAL NAME
Al Jumhuriyah al Lubnaniyah (Lebanese Republic)

FLAG DESCRIPTION
Three horizontal bands of red (top), white (middle, with double width), and red (bottom) with a green cedar tree centered in the white band

CAPITAL
Beirut

ETHNIC GROUPS
Arab 95 percent, Armenian 4 percent, other (Assyrians, Kurds, Palestinians) 1 percent

RELIGIOUS GROUPS
Muslim (Shia, Sunni, Druze, Isma'ilite, Alawite or Nusayri) 59.7 percent, Christian (Catholic, Greek and Armenian Orthodox, Protestant) 39 percent, Others 1.3 percent

BIRTHRATE
18.52 births per 1,000 Lebanese (2006 estimate)

DEATH RATE
6.21 deaths per 1,000 Lebanese (2006 estimate)

AGE STRUCTURE
0–14 years: 26.5 percent
15–64 years: 66.5 percent
65 years and over: 7 percent (2006 estimates)

MAIN LANGUAGES
Arabic (official), French, English, Armenian

LITERACY RATE
People ages 15 and above who can read and write: 87.4 percent (2006 estimate)

NATIONAL HOLIDAYS
New Year's Day (January 1), Armenian Christmas (January 6), Eid al-Adha (date varies), Islamic New Year (date varies), Ashura/Saint Maron's Day (date varies), Prophet Muhammad's Birthday (date varies), Good Friday (March/April), Orthodox Good Friday (March/April), Labor Day (May 1), Martyrs' Day (May 6), Resistance and Liberation Day (May 14), Assumption Day (August 15), Eid al-Fitr (date varies), Independence Day (November 22), Christmas Day (December 25)

LEADERS IN POLITICS
Béchara Khalil el-Khoury: first president of independent Lebanon (1943–52)
Riyad as-Solh: first prime minister of independent Lebanon (1943–45)
Rafiq al-Hariri: first prime minister of the new National Assembly (1992–98)
Émile Lahoud: president since 1998
Fouad Siniora: prime minister since 2005

TIME LINE

IN LEBANON	IN THE WORLD

1100 B.C.
Phoenicians gain independence from Egypt.

875—64 B.C.
Phoenicians become part of the Roman Empire and accept Christianity as a religion.

753 B.C.
Rome is founded.

A.D. 600
Height of Mayan civilization

1098
The first crusader kingdom is established.

1516–1916
Ottoman Turks conquer Greater Syia, which includes Lebanon, Syria, Jordan, and Israel.

1530
Beginning of transatlantic slave trade organized by the Portuguese in Africa.

1789–99
The French Revolution

1914–18
The Ottoman Empire loses to Britain, France, Russia, and the United States in World War I.

1914
World War I begins.

1920
The League of Nations grants Lebanon and Syria to France. The State of Greater Lebanon is established.

1926
First constitution is drafted and the Lebanese Republic is declared.

1939
World War II begins.

1940
Lebanon comes under control of the Vichy French government during World War II.

1941
Lebanon gains independence from France.

1943
November 22 is celebrated as Independence Day as France transfers power to Lebanese government.

1945
Egypt, Syria, Iraq, and Lebanon form the League of Arab States; Lebanon becomes a member of the United Nations.

IN LEBANON	IN THE WORLD
1948	
Palestinian refugees begin arriving in Lebanon after Israel is declared a state.	**1949** The North Atlantic Treaty Organization (NATO) is formed.
	1957 The Russians launch Sputnik.
	1966–69 The Chinese Cultural Revolution
1967 War between Israel and Arab nations. Palestinians use Lebanon as a base of operations against Israel.	
1975–90 Civil war. Israel assumes control of south Lebanon.	**1986** Nuclear power disaster at Chernobyl in Ukraine
1991 Dissolution of all militias, except Hizbollah; Lebanon signs the Treaty of Brotherhood with Syria.	**1991** Breakup of the Soviet Union
1992 Rafiq al-Hariri is elected as prime minister.	
1996 Israelis bomb Hizbollah bases in southern Lebanon and a UN base, killing more than a hundred civilians.	**1997** Hong Kong is returned to China.
1998 Émile Lahoud is sworn in as president.	
2000 Israel withdraws troops from south Lebanon. May 25 declared "Resistance and Liberation Day."	**2001** Terrorists crash planes in New York, Washington, D.C., and Pennsylvania.
2002 Lebanon hosts the Arab League Summit.	
	2003 War in Iraq begins.
2005 Fouad Siniora is elected prime minister after Rafiq al-Hariri is assassinated.	
2006 Israel launches major military attacks in Lebanon after Hizbollah takes hostage two Israeli soldiers.	

GLOSSARY

Abbasid (ah-BAH-sid)
Dynasty of Arab rulers that ruled Lebanon from A.D. 750 to 1250.

arrack (ah-RUCK)
The national drink, a heady liquor distilled from grapes and flavored with anise.

confession
A Lebanese community defined by religion.

Druze (Druse) (DROOS)
A Middle Eastern Muslim sect living mostly in the mountainous regions of Lebanon and Syria.

falafel (fehl-A-fehl)
Spicy, deep-fried balls of chickpea paste mixed with spices and vegetables.

Hizbollah
Radical Muslim organization that continues to oppose Israel.

hummus (HUM-us)
Chickpea paste mixed with lemon, sesame oil, and garlic.

Levant
Countries bordering the eastern shores of the Mediterranean Sea.

Maronites
Uniate Catholics. Originated in Syria in the seventh century, now chiefly found in Lebanon.

meze (meh-ZAY)
Wide-ranging spread of hot and cold appetizers.

militia
A military force, especially one that is formed from the civilian population as a result of an emergency situation.

muezzin (moo-EZ-in)
Mosque official who calls worshippers to prayer.

oud (*'ud*) (OOD)
Stringed musical instrument, forerunner of the European lute.

Phoenician
A seafaring Semitic people of ancient Phoenicia, a land that included modern Lebanon.

Shiites (Shia) (SHE-ites)
An Islamic sect, originating with the murder of Ali, Prophet Muhammad's son-in-law and nephew. The Shiites were supporters of Ali's claim to be the Islamic leader after Muhammad.

Sunni (SOO-nee)
Mainstream Islamic sect throughout the Middle East, making up 80 percent of all Muslims in the world. This group differs from Shiite Muslims in the matter of Prophet Muhammad's successor.

Umayyad (oo-MAY-ahd)
A dynasty of Arab caliphs, based in Damascus, that ruled Lebanon from A.D. 630 to 750.

FURTHER INFORMATION

BOOKS

Al-Shaykh, Hanan. *Beirut Blues.* (Translated by Catherine Cobham) New York: Anchor Books, 1995.

Fisk, Robert. *Pity the Nation: Lebanon at War.* New York: Oxford University Press, 2001.

Gibran, Kahlil. *The Prophet.* London: Penguin, 2002.

Goldstein, Margaret. *Lebanon in Pictures (Visual Geography Series).* Minneapolis, MN: Lerner Publications, 2004.

Goldstein, Margaret J. *Lebanon in Pictures.* Minneapolis, MN: Lerner Publications, 2005.

Haag, Michael. *Syria and Lebanon.* London: Cadogan Books, 1995.

Marston, Elsa. *Figs and Fate: Stories about Growing Up in the Arab World Today.* New York: George Braziller, 2005.

WEB SITES

Beirut Times. www.beiruttimes.com

Central Intelligence Agency World Factbook (select Lebanon from country list). www.cia.gov/cia/publications/factbook

GreenLine. www.greenline.org

Lonely Planet World Guide: Lebanon. www.lonelyplanet.com/worldguide/destinations/middle-east/lebanon

Music of Lebanon. www.musicoflebanon.com

FILMS

60 Minutes: "The New Beirut." CBS, 2006.

Childhood Lost. Icarus Film, 1992.

Children of Shatila. Arab Film Distribution, 1998.

Destination: The Middle East. Pilot Film Productions, 2003.

West Beirut. 38 Productions, ACCI, 1998.

MUSIC

Legendary Fairuz. Blue Note Records, 1998

BIBLIOGRAPHY

Cleary, Thomas (translator). *The Essential Koran*. San Francisco: Harper, 1994.

Foster, Leila Merrell. *Enchantment of the World: Lebanon*. Chicago: Children's Press, 1992.

Frenea, Elizabeth and Robert. *The Arab World: Personal Encounters*. Garden City, NY: Anchor, 1985.

Lebanon in Pictures. Visual Geography Series. Minneapolis, MN: Lerner Publications, 1988.

Maalouf, Amin. *The Crusades Through Arab Eyes*. New York: Schocken Books, 1987.

Marston, Elsa. *Lebanon: New Light in an Ancient Land*. New York: Dillon Press, 1994.

Musallam, Basim. *The Arabs: A Living History*. London: Collins/Harvill, 1983.

Arizona Daily Star Online. www.dailystar.com

Central Administration for Statistics. www.cas.gov.org

Embassy of Lebanon. www.lebanonembassy.org

Lebanese Center for Policy Studies (LCPS). www.lcps-lebanon.org

United Nations. www.un.org

INDEX

143